HOW TO MAKE

MONEY ON FORECLOSURES
Answer Book

Practical Answers to More Than 125 Questions on Investing
in Foreclosure Property

DENISE L. EVANS
ATTORNEY AT LAW

SPHINX® PUBLISHING
AN IMPRINT OF SOURCEBOOKS, INC.®
NAPERVILLE, ILLINOIS
www.SphinxLegal.com

First Edition: 2008

Published by: Sphinx® Publishing, An Imprint of Sourcebooks, Inc.®

<u>Naperville Office</u>
P.O. Box 4410
Naperville, Illinois 60567-4410
630-961-3900
Fax: 630-961-2168
www.sourcebooks.com
www.SphinxLegal.com

This publication is designed to provide accurate and authoritative information in regard to the subject matter covered. It is sold with the understanding that the publisher is not engaged in rendering legal, accounting, or other professional service. If legal advice or other expert assistance is required, the services of a competent profes-sional person should be sought.
From a Declaration of Principles Jointly Adopted by a Committee of the American Bar Association and a Committee of Publishers and Associations

This product is not a substitute for legal advice.

Disclaimer required by Texas statutes

Library of Congress Cataloging-in-Publication Data

Evans, Denise L.
  The make money on foreclosures answer book : practical answers to the top 125 ques-tions on investing in foreclosure property / by Denise L. Evans. -- 1st ed.
     p. cm.
  Includes index.
  ISBN 978-1-57248-649-2 (pbk. : alk. paper) 1. Real estate investment. 2. Foreclosure. I. Title.

HD1382.5.E973 2008
332.63'24--dc22
                                        2007048789

Contents

Foreword v

Chapter 1: Foreclosure Basics 1
Chapter 2: Deciding to Invest in Foreclosures 27
Chapter 3: Establish Your Goals 37
Chapter 4: Finding Appropriate Properties 47
Chapter 5: Understanding the Parties and Their Motivations 63
Chapter 6: Ready, Set, Buy! 79
Chapter 7: Financing Your Purchase 99
Chapter 8: What You Should Know about Taxes 113
Chapter 9: Bankruptcy and Foreclosure 127
Chapter 10: The Former Owner 133
Conclusion 143
Glossary 145
Appendix A: Sample Business Plan 153
Appendix B: HUD Good Neighbor Next Door 159
Appendix C: State-Specific Information 167
Appendix D: Understanding the Real Estate Contract 227
Appendix E: Spreadsheets You Can Use 235

Index 245
About the Author 249

Foreword

According to research conducted by the Center for Responsible Lending, 3.2 million consumers borrowed money under so-called subprime mortgages in 2006. The Center estimates that 19.4% of those loans, or a whopping 624,000 mortgages, will end in foreclosure.

From the website of the Center for Responsible Lending, **www.responsiblelending.org**, and as reported in *Mortgage Servicing News*, "Wanted: Default Relief," by Brian Collins, May 2007, vol. 11, no. 4, page 1.

With so many home mortgages ending up in foreclosure, it is an ideal time to invest in these properties. But, in order to minimize your risk and become a successful investor, you have to know what you are doing and understand the process of investing in foreclosure properties.

In this book, I will explain the process and help you learn how to invest in and make money from foreclosures. I will define the vocabulary terms you need to know, and I will explain how to set up the procedures you need to use to be successful.

One word of caution before we begin. The laws in every state are different. Not only that, but they change very quickly. Check the law in your state on the different issues mentioned in this book.

Good luck!

Chapter 1

FORECLOSURE BASICS

- What is a foreclosure?
- What other sales are similar to foreclosures?
- What causes foreclosures?
- Are owners in foreclosure deadbeats?
- Why do I have to understand the foreclosure process?
- What steps lead up to a foreclosure?
- What is involved in a nonjudicial foreclosure?
- How does a judicial foreclosure work?
- What is a voluntary foreclosure?
- Can a foreclosure be stopped once the process has started?
- What happens to the former owner after foreclosure?
- What happens to tenants after a foreclosure?
- Does a spouse have rights in foreclosed real estate, even if his or her name was not on the deed?
- What happens to other creditors after a foreclosure?
- Who controls the foreclosure process?
- How do I find out who is in control of the foreclosure process?
- What is MERS?
- Can a former owner buy his or her property back after foreclosure?
- How can I separate myth from reality when I learn about foreclosure investing from other sources?
- Can I make money if there are a lot of foreclosures on the market?
- Can I get rich from buying and selling foreclosures?

What is a foreclosure?

Foreclosure is the process in which a lender takes action to *foreclose*—to shut out, to bring to an end—a borrower's rights in real estate. In a foreclosure, the real estate is security for a loan, the borrower defaulted, and now the lender wants to take the property, sell it, and apply the proceeds as a credit against the loan. Strictly speaking, all foreclosures come after there has been a voluntary agreement to borrow money and provide the lender with collateral consisting of a specific piece of real estate.

Other processes result in creditors taking real estate away from debtors. Those will be described in the next question. In this book, I will generally refer to all involuntary losses of property to creditors as *foreclosures*, even though they might technically be separated into foreclosures, judgment executions, tax sales, Internal Revenue Service (IRS) seizures, and bankruptcy auctions, to name a few.

What other sales are similar to foreclosures?

People can lose their ownership of real estate in a wide variety of ways. The most common are as follows.

- *IRS seizures* occur when all real and personal property of the taxpayer is subject to an IRS lien for unpaid taxes. The IRS may pick and choose which assets to sell and in what order to sell them. State and local governments can do the same thing for their own tax bills. This is different from the IRS criminal investigations seizures mentioned later.

- *Real estate tax auctions* arise from unpaid property taxes related to specific real estate. Only the property with the unpaid real estate taxes may be sold. All other properties are safe if their taxes were paid.

- *Judgment executions* occur after one person sues another person and wins a judgment. The lawsuit can be for a debt, injuries from an accident, breach of contract claims, or almost anything at all. The most common theme is a lawsuit and then a money judgment against the defendant. Once all the appeals have been exhausted, the winner—the *judgment creditor*—may seize and sell any of the loser's real or personal property. There are some limitations that we will cover later.

- *Government surplus property auctions* are the most likely foreclosures you might encounter. They occur after the government takes private property under its eminent domain rights, and then auctions off the portions it does not need for the new school, library, etc.

- *Bankruptcy auctions* are required in order to liquidate the debtor's assets and distribute the money among various creditors.

- *United States Marshall's Service forfeiture auctions* sell property seized as a result of criminal activities.

- *United States Treasury Department seizures* occur as a result of criminal investigations by the IRS; Immigration and Customs Enforcement; United States Secret Service; and the Bureau of Alcohol, Tobacco, Firearms, and Explosives.

What causes foreclosures?

Foreclosures, and all the generic-types of involuntary transfers in the prior question (except government surplus auctions), occur because someone did not follow the rules or made unwise decisions.

A borrower did not make his or her payments on time. Someone did not pay his or her taxes. Someone else broke the law. The point is, there was a mess and it resulted in the involuntary transfer of real estate. There are many traps and pitfalls when investing in foreclosure properties because while some of the previous owners' messes are visible on the surface, there are other messes that you cannot see right away. If you are knowledgeable, you can avoid most of the risk and minimize the fallout from the problems that cannot be managed in advance.

Are owners in foreclosure deadbeats?

Absolutely not! When I said earlier that most people in foreclosure made unwise decisions, that does not mean they were deadbeats or unethical. It means that, in 20/20 hindsight, they should have done something differently. Most owners facing foreclosure are honest, ethical, and financially responsible people, but they are in a bind. You can work with most of them, most will make good tenants, and they can even provide valuable assistance in your negotiations with the lender.

Why do people find themselves in these situations? Among the most common reasons are the following.

- People have a lack of adequate health insurance combined with large medical bills. If someone needs continuing medical care, he or she is more likely to try to keep up with health care costs than the mortgage payments.

- Adjustable rate mortgages were affordable when the home was purchased. Now, interest rates have increased significantly, and many people can no longer afford the higher monthly payments.

- People have employment-related circumstances, such as layoffs, long-term disabilities, or job transfers. If you have been transferred to a new job but cannot sell your old house, you might have to let the lender take it.

- Divorce, separation, and death can result in inadequate income to continue making the payments.

- People have spiraling financial problems. Suppose John has some temporary cash flow problems and runs consistently late on his mortgage, credit card, and car payments. His credit score will sink dramatically as a result. Then, when his car needs major repairs, he must come up with the cash for the repairs or trade the car in for another one. John probably does not have the cash, and his poor credit score means the new car will have very high interest rates and high monthly payments. John's financial problems get worse. He needs the car to get to work, so he cannot allow it to be repossessed. In all likelihood, the mortgage payments will suffer.

Once you understand that people in foreclosure arrive there for a variety of perfectly understandable reasons, you are much more able to find them, negotiate with them, and work out solutions to your mutual financial advantage.

Why do I have to understand the foreclosure process?

Once you understand how involuntary transfers occur, you will be much better at spotting opportunities early, ahead of everyone else. You will also have a good appreciation of things that can go wrong at various stages of the foreclosure process that can possibly result in you losing money on your investment. Knowing what can go wrong can help you protect yourself because you will be on the lookout for those types of warnings.

What steps lead up to a foreclosure?

Foreclosures are a specific class of involuntary transfers that have very formalized steps throughout the process. They vary from state to state in the particulars but generally fall into two categories: judicial foreclosures and nonjudicial foreclosures.

Usually, states that employ something called a *deed of trust* as security for real estate loans follow the nonjudicial foreclosure route. Most other states, which use an instrument called a *mortgage*, must go to court in order to complete a judicial foreclosure. Some states use mortgages but also allow nonjudicial foreclosures. To find out about the rules in your state, check Appendix C for resource information.

Generally speaking, a borrower is usually given a certain *grace period* in the loan documents. He or she may catch up on the loan payments within the grace period and suffer no bad consequences. The grace periods vary among states and different lenders. After the grace period expires, the lender will usually send out a *notice of acceleration* to the borrower. The notice says that because of the continuing default in making monthly payments, the lender is now declaring the entire balance of the loan due and payable immediately.

There is then some sort of public notice. It might be a notice in the legal section of the newspaper or on a bulletin board designated for that purpose at the local courthouse. It might be a notation in the real estate records, or the filing of a lawsuit by the lender. That is usually the first indication to potential buyers that a foreclosure is in process.

At some point before the auction, the lender will usually request an updated *title report* on the property. This will confirm the lender's priority among all the possible claimants, such as other mortgages, judgment creditors, or unpaid taxes. The lender might have to give additional notices under the circumstances, such as to the IRS. Or, the lender might re-evaluate the amount of money he or she would be willing to accept at an auction, especially if there are other liens that will remain on the property after a foreclosure.

Normally, the lender will also obtain an updated appraisal or something called a *broker's price opinion* (BPO). The BPO is more common. The lender will contact a local real estate broker and ask that broker for something in writing indicating the price the broker would recommend asking if the property had a listing. As a real estate broker myself, I can tell you that any request for a BPO almost always means a foreclosure will occur. This gives the broker a tremendous advantage—he or she gains early knowledge of a potential foreclosure and already knows the probable value of the property. Unfortunately, the BPO system may lead to abuse of power, as unethical brokers provide very low values, hoping to buy the property themselves or assist a client in bidding at the auction.

The next stage leading up to foreclosure depends on whether the property is in a judicial or a nonjudicial state. Those issues are covered separately as follows.

What is involved in a nonjudicial foreclosure?

Nonjudicial foreclosures are fairly straightforward. They come about because the borrower executed a document—usually a deed of trust—authorizing the sale of the property upon default and satisfaction of all state preforeclosure requirements. After the required notice period has expired, a representative of the lender will usually go to the place designated by law for public sales, which is typically the courthouse steps for the county or parish where the property is located.

State law also usually provides the time period for the legal hours of sale, such as "between one o'clock and four o'clock in the afternoon." You can nail down a more specific time by calling the lender's representative the day before the auction.

Colorado has a hybrid procedure involving public trustees. The governor appoints a public trustee for each county. They are supposed to make sure that the foreclosure takes place in an impartial and fair manner. The public trustee has many responsibilities leading up to the foreclosure and actually conducts the auction. The lender must obtain a court order—after something called a *Rule 120 Proceeding*—before it can go forward with the foreclosure auction. Despite the need for a court order, Colorado foreclosures are considered nonjudicial.

At the appointed time, the auctioneer will read the foreclosure notice. He or she will ask for bids, just like at any other auction. If there are no bids, the auctioneer, or a separate person from the lender's offices, will offer the credit bid amount. Provided there are no other bids, the auctioneer will accept that amount and sell the property to the lender. In the alternative, another bidder might place the highest offer and be awarded the property.

Sometimes the winning bidder must have the funds available to close immediately. Other times, the bidder must make an immediate earnest money deposit in a predetermined percentage and proceed to closing within a certain number of days. The winning bidder usually does not have the benefit of normal purchase contingencies, such as property inspection, good title, or ability to secure financing. Once you pay the earnest money, you must proceed to closing or forfeit the earnest money.

How does a judicial foreclosure work?

Judicial foreclosures require a court order to take place because the lending documents do not give the lender the right to sell the property. Usually, this means the parties executed a mortgage rather than a deed of trust, although some mortgages also contain powers of sale.

In a judicial foreclosure, the lender must file a lawsuit against the borrower and also name all the other parties who might have an interest in the property. Other parties might include other creditors, the borrower's spouse, tenants of the owner, and similar persons. The lender must obtain *service* on each party, which means the court papers must be delivered in a particular way and normally to a particular person. Simply mailing copies of the lawsuit is usually not enough.

The lender also files something called a *lis pendens* in the real estate records where deeds are recorded. The *lis pendens* is a notice that the creditor has filed suit in order to foreclose on the property. If the owner sells the property to someone else after the lis pendens has been filed, the buyer is considered to have been put on notice that foreclosure has started. The buyer cannot complain when foreclosure takes place and he or she ends up owning nothing.

Each party then has a certain number of days to file an *answer*. An answer might contest the foreclosure itself, or might claim that a party has rights that are superior to those of the foreclosing lender. An answer might also consist of a simple acknowledgment that the lender has the right to proceed as it is doing, and the party has no dispute with that action.

If the borrower does not answer, the court might require the appointment of a referee to determine the amount due. If the borrower does answer, then each party will present arguments regarding its version of the amount due, and the court will decide the actual amount that is due.

In some states, the court will establish a minimum value for the property. If there are no higher bids at auction, the creditor must buy the property at the preset value and give the borrower a credit in that amount.

After all the disputes have been resolved, if foreclosure is still warranted, the court will enter an *order of foreclosure*. That order is not the foreclosure itself. An auction must then take place. The borrower still owns the property up until the auction and the delivery of a deed to the auction buyer.

What is a voluntary foreclosure?

A *voluntary foreclosure* is a simplified method of turning property over to the creditor by the borrower. Sometimes it is called a *private foreclosure*. It is also sometimes called a *deed in lieu of foreclosure*, although the two might be different things in some states.

There are several benefits to all concerned. Many states allow a deficiency judgment against the borrower after a foreclosure. In other words, if the auction does not bring enough money to satisfy the debt, the lender can still obtain a judgment against the borrower for the balance due, and then execute on other assets or garnish the debtor's wages. The voluntary foreclosure removes that possibility, and the creditor accepts the property as payment in full for the debt.

Some states give the former owner the right to buy his or her property back for some time period after a regular foreclosure. This is called a *right of redemption*. The purchase price is set at the amount of the foreclosure bid, plus interest and some expenses. A voluntary foreclosure results in the borrower giving up the right of redemption. As a result, the lender can take steps to sell the property immediately, without the market being chilled by outstanding rights of redemption.

Often, if you can work out a deal with the borrower and lender prior to the auction, they will elect to do a voluntary foreclosure.

Can a foreclosure be stopped once the process has started?

In all circumstances, the lender itself can stop the foreclosure process midstride. Some states allow the auction to be resumed at a later date after the publication of some sort of notice. Other states require the lender to start all over again. It is easier to negotiate with lenders in states that allow brief interruptions without starting over because the lender knows it can resume foreclosure if negotiations break down.

Many states give the borrower, and sometimes junior lienholders, the ability to *cure* the default and stop foreclosure. When allowed, curing takes place by catching up all the past due payments and reimbursing the creditor for all its preforeclosure expenses up to that point. States that allow this right have different time periods for the cure. Refer to Appendix C for more details.

Bankruptcy will also stop the foreclosure process. We will cover this in more detail later because a good understanding of bankruptcy is essential for any foreclosure investor. At this point, it is enough to know that many foreclosures stopped by bankruptcy are merely delayed and not completely stopped. You can continue to monitor the debtor's progress, and you may have an opportunity to purchase the property at a later date.

What happens to the former owner after foreclosure?

The fate of the former owner varies from state to state. In some, the auction purchaser—whether it is the lender or a third party—sends notice that the former owner must vacate the premises. If the former owner does not surrender possession within the legal time limits, he or she could lose valuable rights to buy back the property at a later date.

Other states allow the former owner to occupy the foreclosed property for up to one year. Still other states take the position that a foreclosure is the end of everything for the former owner. He or she has no right of occupancy, no right to buy the property back, and no right to reverse the foreclosure, even if it was wrongful. The former owner's sole remedy is to sue the lender for money damages.

Make sure you know the rules of your particular state before purchasing a foreclosure property. The different rules could make a dramatic difference in your decision making. Appendix C provides a good overview of state laws and also gives resources for more information.

Another postforeclosure issue has to do with *deficiency judgments*. What happens when the property is worth less than the outstanding balance on the loan? There are two possibilities.

1. The lender may obtain a deficiency judgment against the borrower for the remaining balance on the loan. This is the same as any other judgment. It can be collected by the seizure of other assets, the garnishment of wages, or the garnishment of bank accounts.

2. The lender is not allowed to obtain a deficiency judgment, but must be satisfied with the real estate alone.

The rules differ among states, and also according to the actual loan agreements between the lender and borrower.

When a lender agrees up front that it will look to the real estate for its recovery in the event of a default and the borrower will have no personal liability, it is called *nonrecourse lending*. Even in states that allow deficiency judgments, a nonrecourse loan agreement protects the borrower against any further liability.

What happens to tenants after a foreclosure?

This is a really important question because you might buy a piece of real estate at foreclosure, only to find out someone else is entitled to live there for the next several years, rent free! How does that happen?

Suppose the owner of a house signs a written ten-year lease agreement with her son. The son will maintain the house, make all repairs, and pay all insurance and taxes. The rent is $1 per year, and the son prepays the entire ten-year term by writing his mother a check for $10 and noting on it, "Payment in full for ten years' rent on 123 Main Street."

One year later the mother borrows $25,000 and gives a mortgage on the house. Another year later she defaults, the bank forecloses, and you buy the house at the foreclosure auction. The son has another eight years left on his lease. Can you kick out the son, or are you stuck for the next eight years, with no right to occupancy and no rental income? In almost all states, if the lease was signed before the mortgage, then the foreclosure does not wipe out the lease. It still exists, and the foreclosure buyer must honor the terms of the lease. Check Appendix C for landlord/tenant resources in your state, and be sure to satisfy yourself on this issue.

Sometimes lenders will require preexisting tenants to sign subordination agreements. In real estate, a *subordination agreement* means an agreement to go under someone else's rights. In this case, a tenant might agree that his or her rights are subordinate to those of a mortgage lender, even though the lease was signed first. If there is a foreclosure, the tenant's rights will come to an end because of the subordination agreement.

The more typical case is when the mortgage is signed before the lease. In that instance, when the landlord's rights end because of foreclosure, the tenant's rights also end.

When investigating foreclosure properties, always ask about the possibility of tenants having rights. If the mortgage money was used to purchase the property, then obviously there could be no prior tenants. In all other instances, you will have to ask questions about this issue.

Does a spouse have rights in foreclosed real estate, even if his or her name was not on the deed?

In most states, a spouse has some sort of rights in real estate, even if his or her name is not on the deed. Those rights might arise because of community property laws, something called *dower and curtesy*, which is a surviving spouse's right to receive a set portion of a deceased spouse's estate—*homestead protections* or *survivorship protections*.

It is important to know your state's laws, because you do not want to buy foreclosed real estate and then find out you have a co-owner—the spouse of the former owner.

What happens to other creditors after a foreclosure?

Creditors who have rights in real estate are called *lienholders*. They might gain those rights through other mortgages, judgment liens, tax liens, mechanics' and materialmen's (M&M) liens, or as a result of divorce. By and large, with the exception of real estate taxes and possibly M&M liens, any lien that was recorded after the mortgage was foreclosed will be canceled by the foreclosure.

Most states give a super priority to *real estate tax liens*. This is a lien for unpaid real estate taxes, not to be confused with IRS tax liens. Usually, real estate tax liens stay on property no matter what happens. *Mechanics' and materialmen's liens* arise because of unpaid bills after work is performed for the benefit of the real estate. Many states allow the mechanics' and materialmen's lien to be filed after a mortgage but still give superior rights to the mortgage lender. If that happens, the lienholder must usually take steps to foreclose on the lien within a very short period of time— usually six months—or lose the lien.

In the following example, I have illustrated which liens will survive a foreclosure. Even after a foreclosure sale, the liens that survive will still be on the property. That lienholder can then conduct its own foreclosure and take the property away from the successful buyer without paying any compensation to the buyer.

Jan. 1	Mortgage to 1st Federal Lenders
Feb. 1	Mortgage to 2nd Federal Lenders
March 1	IRS lien
July 1	Judgment lien by hospital creditor
Sept. 1	New roof installed by Rex Roofers
Oct. 1	Real estate taxes are due
Nov. 1	2nd Federal forecloses; you buy
Dec. 1	Rex Roofers files lien for unpaid bill

It is very likely that your property will still be subject to the 1st Federal Lenders mortgage, the real estate taxes, and the Rex Roofers lien for the unpaid roofing bill. If 2nd Federal Lenders did not give the proper specialized written notice to the IRS, that lien will also remain, even though this company filed after the 1st Federal Lenders mortgage.

Because of the danger of liens remaining on property after a foreclosure, it is extremely important to order a *title commitment* before obligating yourself to buy the property. A title commitment can be obtained through almost any real estate closing company. Ask a real estate agent for some names if you do not already know a company.

The title commitment is much less expensive than a full title policy. The *title commitment* is the insurance company's commitment to issue a title policy once closing takes place and the deed to you has been recorded. When ordering, you should advise the company that you want a commitment for title insurance after a particular lender has foreclosed. The title commitment will list all other possible claimants to the property and require that those parties' claims be released as a condition of issuing title insurance. This will give you an early warning of postforeclosure problems.

Chapter 5 will answer questions about negotiating with lienholders. It can be done successfully, but first you have to know who they are ahead of time. Once you buy the property, it is probably too late to start negotiating because you are no longer in a position of strength.

Who controls the foreclosure process?

You might think the lender controls the foreclosure process, but things are not quite that simple. Let us look at Robin Smith, a typical mortgage borrower. Robin borrowed $145,000 from her local hometown bank, 1st National. Most likely, 1st National will then sell the mortgage to someone else, a company that buys loans from lenders all over the United States. The largest buyers are *Fannie Mae* (Federal National Mortgage Association), *Ginnie Mae* (Government

National Mortgage Association), and *Freddie Mac* (Federal Home Loan Mortgage Corporation). Private investment firms also purchase loans. For this example, we will call one such firm Acme Investors.

Robin might continue to receive statements from 1st National even though Acme Investors bought her loan. Or, she might receive statements from yet a third party, a loan servicing company we will call Loan Servicers.

Suppose Robin loses her job and will not be able to make her mortgage payments. She is facing foreclosure. You want to work something out with her and with the lender to buy the property before foreclosure. Who do you talk to, and how much authority does he or she have to negotiate with you? This issue alone—who you talk to—probably accounts for most people becoming discouraged and dropping out of preforeclosure investing.

The *servicing company* usually controls the foreclosure process and any negotiations to avoid foreclosure. In our example, Loan Servicers might have a great deal of latitude in working out a solution with you. Or, they might have no discretion at all because their hands are tied under the servicing contract they signed with Acme Investors.

If Loan Servicers is not allowed to control the process, but merely put into motion preapproved steps leading to foreclosure, then Acme Investors probably does not control anything meaningful, either. I know that does not make sense because we said that Acme Investors owned the loan. Surely, you would think, the owner can exercise control and work with you to find a solution that would result in more money than a foreclosure would generate.

You have to remember that Acme owns many thousands or millions of loans. It is not cost effective for them to spend hours working with you and completing all the necessary internal paperwork, just to receive a little more money than an auction would yield. Also, Acme has investors to whom it has sold bonds that are backed up by mortgages such as Robin's. Because of Acme's responsibilities to its bond holders, it might be safer for it to do nothing and let the foreclosure proceed to auction, rather than depart from routine and possibly end up in a worse financial position.

For the most part, servicing companies and large investment companies are bureaucracies. It is common wisdom inside a bureaucracy that following the rules will never get you in trouble, even if it results in a stupid and wasteful outcome. Not following the rules can result in punishment if the outcome is bad, but it can result in the same thing even if the outcome is good. There is no incentive to work creatively to find solutions. That is the problem with bureaucracies.

The short answer is that you might find out that no one truly controls the foreclosure process. Once Robin defaults, everyone might be on a runaway freight train headed toward a foreclosure auction. If you try to control it, you will just make yourself crazy before you finally become discouraged. Instead of doing that, find out early if anyone is in control, who that party is, and how much discretion he or she has.

How do I find out who is in control of the foreclosure process?

You have two avenues to find this information—either the borrower will tell you the name of the servicing company, or you have to find out by yourself.

It is usually better to work with the full knowledge and assistance of the borrower when trying to buy preauction foreclosure properties. State and federal privacy laws prevent the lender from telling you anything at all, which makes it very difficult to negotiate. The borrower can tell you how to contact the servicing company.

Without the borrower's help, you will almost never be able to identify the servicing company unless it also happens to be the lender that originated the mortgage. Start with that company. Next, check the local real estate records to see if it *assigned* (sold) the mortgage to another company. One of the clerks in the real estate records room of your parish or county can help you with the search procedures. Often, you can search real estate records online.

If the mortgage lender is showing up as MERS, the following question will help you find the true party with whom you can negotiate.

What is MERS?

MERS is short for *Mortgage Electronic Registration System*. The company was created by the mortgage loan industry in order to streamline the process of creating mortgage loans and then selling them to investors. It is also heavily engaged in the system for the electronic registration and tracking of promissory notes nationwide.

Formerly, if 1st National Bank sold a mortgage to Acme Investors, two things would have to happen. In the case of Robin, in our prior example, 1st National would send Robin's original promissory note to Acme Investors. This would require delivery fees plus insurance in case the note were lost. In addition, 1st National would have to file something in the real estate records showing that the mortgage or deed of trust had been assigned to Acme, which would also cost money. There would also be a lot of room for human error in failing to do things or doing them incorrectly.

MERS was created to solve this problem. Members can execute mortgages in the name of MERS as the nominee. For example, Robin's loan money might have come from 1st National, but her note and mortgage might say she owes the money to MERS as the nominee. In addition, her mortgage or deed of trust will name MERS (as the nominee) as the secured party.

MERS can be the nominee for anyone without him or her having to

send documents through the mail, buy insurance, or change information in the real estate records. When 1st National sells Robin's loan to
Acme Investors, MERS computers will show that it is now the nominee
for Acme Investors instead of 1st National Bank. A few clicks on the
keyboard, and everything else happens automatically. It is a very
streamlined, efficient, and economical system. Foreclosures are
conducted in the name of MERS, but anyone in the world might be the
actual owner of the note and mortgage, and the one calling the shots.

You can identify the servicing company for the mortgage loan in
the following manner. Call MERS at (888) 679-6377 or go to its web
page at **www.mers-servicerid.org**. By calling the toll-free number, you
can enter the eighteen-digit *Mortgage Identification Number* (MIN)
and hear an automated reply with the name and contact information
of the servicer. The website will let you obtain the same information
by using the MIN, borrower name, or property address.

Mortgage

MIN 1234567-8901234567-8

This MORTGAGE is made this 31st day of December, 2007
between the Grantor Robin Smith, herein "Borrower," and the
Mortgagee, Mortgage Electronic Registration Systems, Inc.
("MERS"), (solely as a nominee for Lender, as hereinafter
defined, and Lender's successors and assigns.) MERS is organized and exists under the laws of Delaware, and has an address
and telephone number of P.O. Box 2026, Flint, MI,
48501-2026, tel. (888) 679-MERS. Countrywide Bank, FSB,
A Federal Savings Bank ("Lender") is organized and exists
under The laws of the United States and has an address of
1199 North Fairfax Street, Suite 500, Alexandria, VA 22314.

I find there is usually less opportunity for error if you use the MIN. It is located on the first page of the mortgage, preceded by the letters "MIN." An example appears below:

Can a former owner buy his or her property back after foreclosure?

Of course the former owner can always buy his or her property back on the same terms and conditions you are offering to sell it to third parties. The real question is, can the former owner force you to sell the property back to him or her for a price approximately equal to what he or she owed on the loan, rather than the full market value? The answer to this question depends on the state in which the property is located.

This right is generally called the *right of redemption*. Some states use that phrase to mean the right of a borrower to catch up his or her loan before foreclosure and stop the whole process. Other states use the expression to mean the borrower's right to pay off the mortgage loan after the foreclosure court order, but before something called a *law day*. It can get a little confusing. The rules in your state can be found in Appendix C.

The details of the right of redemption also vary from state to state. In my state, for example, the borrower, and any creditors of the borrower, may redeem the property for up to one year after the foreclosure. In other states the right of redemption can be as short as three months. The Colorado seventy-five-day right of redemption is being phased out as of January 1, 2008. The redemption price is the foreclosure purchase price, plus interest, and reimbursement for some expenses such as taxes and insurance.

If your state has a postforeclosure right of redemption, you can sometimes force a cancellation of those rights, or you can buy them from the former owner. We will cover the details and the specific questions regarding negotiating with the former owner in Chapter 5.

How can I separate myth from reality when I learn about foreclosure investing from other sources?

My overall rule of thumb is: "If it sounds too good to be true, it usually is unless I can personally confirm otherwise." Aside from that general advice, here are a few of the more common foreclosure myths, and the truth of the situations:

- **Myth:** You can get rich buying and selling foreclosures.

  Truth: Only a very few, very dedicated, and very lucky people get rich buying and selling foreclosures. Your odds are probably better in Las Vegas. The truth is, you can make some good investments, you can find a home at a discounted price, and you can supplement your income or even provide yourself with a comfortable living in foreclosures. Depending on how you define it, getting rich is only a reality for the tiniest minority.

- **Myth:** Only modest homes in poor condition are foreclosed.

  Truth: Foreclosures respect no boundaries when it comes to income levels and values of homes. The upper class, lower class, and middle class all have members who live beyond their means, and many members who suffer economic setbacks in their jobs or have unexpected expenses that take all their money. The borrowers are generally not financially irresponsible, and their properties are usually in good condition. They have been good homeowners, they are willing to make sensible choices, and they will work with you if you can provide them with some solutions.

- **Myth:** Foreclosed homes can be purchased at deep discounts of 50% or more.

  Truth: This is rarely true. Yes, in former days most home loans were 80% of the value of the home, and the borrower probably also made some principal reductions with his or her regular payments before the default. If you could buy the home for the payoff on the loan, you might get something at 75% to 80% of the market value. Today, many foreclosures are for loans of 100%—or more—of the value of the home. Some company such as the Federal Housing Administration (FHA) or Guaranty Mortgage Insurance Corporation will guarantee the loan so the borrower can obtain more than 80% of the value. That insurance company will take a loss if the property sells for less than fair market value. These companies are very creative, and very good at finding solutions that return the highest sale price possible.

- **Myth:** We are on the brink of seeing massive numbers of foreclosures, creating incredible opportunities for investors.

  Truth: As I write this book, the subprime market meltdown is the most recent boogeyman feeding this myth. There have been many more over the years. First, economic downturns are rarely as bad as predicted, usually because of the large number and variety of brakes that can be applied to the system. Second, if everyone is being foreclosed, who are you going to sell your purchases to? Sure, you can rent them out to former homeowners who still need a place to live, but market rents will also decrease dramatically if things are that bad nationwide. Massive numbers of foreclosures will depress the entire real estate market, increasing your risks and decreasing your profits. What is best for you is a steady stream of moderate numbers of foreclosures.

Can I make money if there are a lot of foreclosures on the market?

You can still make money if your market is flooded with foreclosures. The trick is to find the unique and desirable homes. Otherwise, you are competing with every other house on the market. We say that you are dealing in *fungible goods*—everything is pretty much the same as everything else. The only way you can compete effectively in fungible goods is to slash your price. As an investor, you always want to avoid that situation.

That being said, there is one other way to maintain profits when buying and selling fungible goods. That is the Chiquita Banana approach. Chiquita puts a little sticker on all their bananas, so you know they are special. They are Chiquita-brand bananas. They look and taste like all other bananas, but that sticker adds value and commands a higher price.

If you can do something similar with foreclosure homes, you can enjoy the same results. Perhaps you can brand your homes as "Joe Jones Certified Homes." You advertise, "I'm Joe Jones and I stand behind every home I sell. If there is a problem after the sale, I live right here in the community. You can find me. I'm not like all those foreclosing lenders who just want to unload inventory. Buy from me, Joe Jones, your neighbor."

Can I get rich from buying and selling foreclosures?

See the first myth previously discussed. Yes, you can get rich, but only in the same way you can get rich in any other business you start. You have to work smart, work hard, and work long. Invest in your business, keep at it consistently, and you will build true wealth over the years.

Do not waste your time looking for the $1 million property you can buy for $100,000 and flip in three months. It will not happen. No homeowner is going to let that much equity go up in smoke. So-called *hard money lenders* will get there before you. They loan money at very high interest rates and for short terms to property owners with cash flow problems but substantial equity in their real estate. The homeowners either pull out of their tailspin, or the hard money lender takes the property, usually in some sort of a private foreclosure.

I suggest you create a business plan for yourself. It will provide a road map for your foreclosure investing and lead to true wealth over time. There is a business plan example in Appendix A.

Over the course of fifteen years and one foreclosure per year, modest flips with $25,000 profits can build a nest egg of $375,000.

Armed with this introductory knowledge, and keeping in mind your own goals, let us get started with foreclosure investing.

Chapter 2

DECIDING TO INVEST IN FORECLOSURES

- What are the benefits of foreclosure investing over other investment vehicles?
- What are the disadvantages of buying foreclosures?
- What are the dangers in buying foreclosures?
- Can I minimize my risks in buying foreclosures?
- What do I need to know about the different types of property I might invest in to further minimize my risks?
- How does title insurance protect me, and when should I buy it?
- Am I the right person for foreclosure investing?

What are the benefits of foreclosure investing over other investment vehicles?

Careful foreclosure shoppers can almost always buy properties at less than full market value. The size of the discount will depend on local market conditions and your own skill, but there are always bargains to be had.

Another benefit is the fact that there is less competition among buyers for foreclosure properties than other investments. Right this very minute, if I had a three-bedroom, two-bathroom, brick ranch-style home in a good school district and in move-in condition, at a reasonable market price, I could sell it to an investor in three minutes. If I had twenty such houses, I could sell all twenty in a day because they make great rental houses. Those same investors to whom I sold the houses would not search out those opportunities among foreclosures. It requires too much work and involves some risk other than the normal economic risks for any investment. There is a lot of competition searching for the *For Sale By Owner* (FSBO) and *Multiple Listing Service* (MLS) rental home candidates. Relatively few investors and future homeowners, by comparison, search the foreclosures.

Another benefit is the ready-made tenant. If your strategy is to buy foreclosures and rent them to the former owners, you will probably have long-term tenants in place. Remember, most former owners were not financially irresponsible. Most of them simply fell on hard times and could not dig themselves out of the hole they were in. You have probably read other books and articles with horror stories about renting to former owners. You should be mindful that such things could happen to you. You could also make millions over the course of a few years by investing in foreclosure houses. Neither one of those things is very likely to happen, although each is possible.

What are the disadvantages of buying foreclosures?

The major disadvantage is the thing that also cuts down the competition—buying foreclosures takes a lot of time. You will have to look at many properties in order to find a home that is right for your needs. Once you find something, your competition comes not just from the other buyers, but from the owners as well. At the last possible moment, they might file for bankruptcy, work something out with the lender, or borrow the money needed from a relative. Then, you would have to start all over, looking for another property.

One important disadvantage is psychological. If your strategy is to search out preforeclosures, or to shop at foreclosure auctions, your sympathy for the owner might cloud your judgment. You will either feel guilty and abandon the strategy, or you will pay too much for the property. You have to remember that this is a business. You can behave ethically and fairly, but that does not mean losing sight of your own interests. People who are able to walk that line will be able to continue. Those who cannot should switch to buying properties *after* the foreclosure, when things are more impersonal.

What are the dangers in buying foreclosures?

The two largest dangers in foreclosure properties are paying too much and buying property that is still subject to other claims.

Paying too much is a common risk any time you enter a situation thinking you will automatically receive a significant discount. You have to know the value of things, and you have to shop wisely.

Real estate agents selling foreclosed properties like to advertise them with the word *foreclosure* plastered over half the photo of the house. That is because people are attracted to such ads. Buyers automatically assume the advertised price is a bargain. In reality, most foreclosed real estate is offered for sale at its appraised value, or in accordance with something called a *broker price opinion* (BPO).

Some brokers will quote a low value in their BPO, hoping to get the listing, and then make a quick sale and a fast commission. Buyers should never assume the listed price is a discounted price.

Many people pay too much at auctions. Their competitive juices kick in and override their common sense. In the alternative, they fall victim to something called the *validation syndrome*, which works like this. Ken thinks a house being foreclosed is worth $125,000 at the most. He plans for that to be his highest bid. At the auction, there are four bidders—Ken, Elsie, Rhonda, and Zack. The bidding is spirited and soon reaches $125,000. Elsie bids $127,500, Zack bids $130,000, and Rhonda bids $132,500. Ken thinks, "If they all think the house is worth more than $125,000, then it must truly be worth more than I thought." Ken bids $135,000, which is $10,000 more than he originally intended to bid.

Ken should not have allowed the other people's bids to *validate* the higher value for the house. The other bidders might simply be wrong because they did not know the market. Elsie might be buying a home for herself and is willing to pay a higher price than an investor. Zack might have other rental houses in the neighborhood and knows he can save money on insurance and maintenance as a result. Rhonda might have sold another property recently and needs to buy something right away to avoid a large income tax bill. If Ken is the winning bidder at $135,000, he probably paid too much.

You might also pay too much because you do not know the condition of the interior of a house, and it turns out to be completely trashed. Obviously, if you are working with owners for preforeclosure purchases, you have an opportunity to inspect the home. Buyers of postforeclosure houses can inspect them before buying. It is only the auction buyers who are buying something unknown. You can guess at the condition of the interior by driving by and looking at the outside. People rarely maintain their lawns if the interior of the house is falling apart. Aside from that, you have to guess at the condition and set your maximum foreclosure bid at a level consistent with the risk you are taking.

The other danger is the risk that the property is still subject to other claims. You run this risk any time you buy any property at all. How do you know the seller is the one entitled to sell the property, no other persons have to sign the deed, and all creditors will be paid out of sale proceeds so that there are no liens on the property? You never know this for sure. All real estate lenders require title insurance to protect their interests. The title insurance company researches these issues before writing the policy, and problems are usually disclosed before closing. If some problem has been overlooked, and there are other claims, then the title insurance company hires lawyers to defend the buyer, or it pays off the other claimants.

Although lenders always require title insurance, many buyers do not request that their interests also be protected. There is an additional premium, but it is well worth the risk. We discuss this issue further in the next two questions.

Can I minimize my risks in buying foreclosures?

You can avoid the most common foreclosure dangers by knowing your market and prevailing prices, doing some detective work to determine the condition of a home, and always buying title insurance.

Remember, also, that a cheap price may not overcome a poor buying decision. People searching for a home of their own should be mindful of all the same factors as they would if they were looking at regular properties. Investors interested in rental income still need to check out market rents for the area, estimate vacancy rates for comparable properties, and calculate annual expenses. Flippers will need to prepare repair and rehab budgets if necessary, advertising and marketing expenses, and holding costs until a resale.

What do I need to know about the different types of property I might invest in to further minimize my risk?

While nothing is guaranteed, here is some information you should know about the different types of foreclosure properties you might purchase.

- *Single-family residential rental property.* Single-family residential homes are easier to sell to another investor, especially if you have a good tenant in place with a lot of time left on the lease.

- *Owner-occupier residential.* It is also possible to sell a single-family home to a person who wants to buy it in order to live in it. You can probably sell the house for a higher price this way.

- *Multi-family residential rental property.* These types of property are good investment properties because they are easier to manage since they are all in one place, and you can also usually receive a higher rate of return on your investment, especially if you manage them yourself.

- *Commercial property.* If you purchase a commercial property to rent out, you will find that the turnover rates tend to be much lower than for residential rental property. Also, you can usually make the commercial tenant pay all of the ownership expenses—like taxes, insurance, and maintenance—if you have a triple net lease with the tenant.

How does title insurance protect me, and when should I buy it?

Title insurance companies will guarantee that you have good title to your real estate, subject to no other claims. If someone else claims to own some interest in the property, the insurance company will either pay the legal fees to contest that claim, or it will pay off the claimant. It works the same way with liens. If there is title insurance and the IRS says it has a $40,000 lien on your property because of past due taxes of the former owner, the title insurance company will pay the $40,000 to obtain a release of the lien.

All real estate lenders require title insurance as a condition of funding their loans. You actually buy the policy at closing on the real estate. The buyer pays the one-time premium as part of the closing costs. What most buyers do not realize is that their equity in the property is not covered by the lender's title insurance. In other words, the buyer must request, and pay the premium for, owner's title insurance.

To illustrate this, suppose Karen buys a postforeclosure property for $80,000. She pays $16,000 down, and finances $64,000 with 1st National. She pays for the lender's title insurance, but does not obtain owner's coverage. Three months after closing, the IRS reveals that it had a lien on the property for $100,000, and the foreclosure did not erase its lien. It wants to seize the property and sell it because it thinks it can find a buyer for $100,000. The title insurance company will pay 1st National $64,000, the full amount of the claim. Karen has no title insurance of her own. Karen will simply lose her $16,000 because the IRS will be able to seize the property and pay her nothing.

It does you no good to secure title insurance at closing if the policy says it will not insure against certain things, such as a $100,000 IRS lien. Most foreclosure sellers will not give you any promises or warranties that they have good title to sell to you. The most they will promise is that they, personally, have done nothing to mess up the title. They advise you of this by saying they will transfer title by *special warranty deed*. The typical deed in most normal circumstances is a *general warranty deed*. You are supposed to know that a *special warranty deed* means the lender is not making any promises.

If you are the winning bidder at auction, or if you sign a contract to buy a postforeclosure property, you may not be able to cancel if you find out there is a $100,000 IRS lien, to use the previous example. Clearly, an early warning system is necessary. That early warning system is a title commitment.

The *title commitment* says that the title insurance company will issue a policy insuring your title if certain specifically described issues—such as a $100,000 IRS lien—are cleared up before closing. This gives you a sneak peak at the title defects if there are any. You can then make an informed decision about whether to proceed to auction or sign a contract at that point.

Am I the right person for foreclosure investing?

All foreclosure strategies require that you be able to assess the market values of properties. A normal nonforeclosure purchase contract usually has a contingency for the buyer being able to obtain acceptable financing. If you agree to pay too much, the lender's appraiser will clue you in pretty quickly, and you will not qualify for financing. It is a sort of safety net for you. You do not have this safety net when buying preforeclosures or when buying at auction. Normally you *do* have it when buying postforeclosure properties.

Other than that overall consideration, the following are the character traits important for various foreclosure strategies.

To purchase preforeclosures, you must be:

- resourceful;

- organized;

- outgoing;

- able to remain detached when faced with others' problems;

- a good negotiator;

- not easily discouraged;

- very goal-oriented; and,

- self-motivated.

To purchase properties at auction, you must be:

- organized;

- disciplined; and,

- willing to take some risk.

To purchase postforeclosures, you must be:

- patient (the best buys are after the property has been on the market for over six months); and,

- not easily discouraged.

Chapter 3

ESTABLISH YOUR GOALS

- Can I buy a home for myself?
- Why can it be so difficult to buy a home to use as my personal residence?
- Are there specialized programs for homeowners to buy foreclosed properties?
- What are the traps for homeowner buyers?
- Should flippers be mindful of any special considerations?
- What sort of Plan B should a flipper have in case the market takes a downturn?
- If my goal is to build a portfolio of rental properties, do foreclosures present any special opportunities?
- How do I invest in redemptory rights?
- Some people recommend reselling to the former owner rather than renting to the former owner. How is that done?

Can I buy a home for myself?

There is no reason you cannot shop foreclosure properties for your personal home buying. However, understand that buying a home for you personal use can make it one of the most difficult properties to purchase. Keep in mind that purchasing a home is an emotional decision. Factors such as pressure from friends and family, the desire for better circumstances for children, and a need to show yourself as established and grown-up may cloud your judgment. Avoid paying too much or taking unnecessary risks by clearly outlining your goals, restrictions, and strategies early. Set a budget and establish realistic expectations for what that budget will buy. Then, stick to your budget and do not pay more money or accept fewer features than originally planned. The only exception is if you find that your original projections were unrealistic; in that case, re-evaluate the entire marketplace, not just the one property you want to buy today.

Why can it be so difficult to buy a home to use as my personal residence?

There are three reasons for this.

1. Buying a home is an emotional decision, not just a practical one. While you can do all the analysis I suggest when looking for a foreclosed home to buy, you are still going to have opinions on the layout of the house, the architectural style, the neighborhood, and even the appliances contained in the house. This can cause you to throw out your financial and neighborhood analyses for emotional reasons and end up with a deal that is not as good.

2. When you purchase a home to live in, you tend to live with a bad decision longer because you do not want to have to pack up

everything and move again. It makes you a lot more cautious when you are looking for a home to purchase. With an investment property, on the other hand, it's a lot easier to sell the house to someone else and move on to a new project.

3. The number of acceptable houses available is smaller when you are looking for a home for use as your personal residence. You need to find a house in the right school system, a house with the best resale value over time, businesses nearby—like a grocery store or post office, and a house near your office so your commute isn't too long. When you purchase a property to sell, these things do not matter.

Are there specialized programs for homeowners to buy foreclosed properties?

There is indeed a variety of specialized programs to help homeowners buy foreclosed real estate. One of the most widely known is the U.S. Department of Housing and Urban Development's *Good Neighbor Next Door* program. Qualified persons in certain professions can buy foreclosures owned by the Department of Housing and Urban Development (HUD) at 50% off the list price. Only certain homes are eligible. They are all in HUD-designated *revitalization areas*. You must live in the home for thirty-six months, but you are free to sell it or turn it into rental property after that. For more details, go to the HUD website at **www.hud.gov/offices/hsg/ sfh/reo/goodn/gnndabot.cfm** or call the local HUD office listed in your telephone white pages.

State and local governments may sponsor similar programs for their own foreclosed or seized real estate. The HUD housing counselors located in your state can help you with information about other programs. See Appendix C for contact information.

What are the traps for homeowner buyers?

There are not really any traps, just things that might not have occurred to you. You probably already know that you can generally obtain conventional financing for 80% of the value of your home. That is the usual loan-to-value ratio when you do not have Federal Housing Administration (FHA) insurance, a Veterans Administration (VA) guarantee, or private mortgage insurance. The word *value* is a little misleading, though. Typical loan commitments offer to finance 80% of the value or 80% of the purchase price, whichever is less.

You might think that you can buy a $100,000 home for $80,000 at foreclosure and obtain 100% financing. This would be a reasonable assumption if you thought you could borrow 80% of the value—$100,000—which works out to $80,000. Instead, you will be able to borrow only 80% of the actual purchase price, which amounts to $64,000. If your goals depend on being able to obtain 100% financing because of buying foreclosure properties at bargain prices, you may find that extremely difficult to do.

If this is your situation, you may need to investigate FHA insurance, VA guarantees, or private mortgage insurance. All three will increase your fees or your monthly payments.

The HUD Good Neighbor Next Door program might also be for you if you have no down payment money. The purchase price of those homes is actually the full listed price. That listed price determines the purchase price for purposes of obtaining 80% financing. The nice thing is, the HUD will accept 50% of the list price as the initial payment, and you sign what is called a *silent second mortgage* to HUD for the other 50%. After three years, if you have met all the requirements, then HUD forgives the second mortgage.

Should flippers be mindful of any special considerations?

Flippers should know the postforeclosure *redemption rights* in their state. It will be very difficult to sell a property at anything close to fair market value if the former owner has the right to repurchase it for the foreclosure bid price.

Suppose Brian's house is foreclosed at a time when it is worth $110,000. The bank buys it for $85,000. A few months later the bank sells the house to Chris for $85,000. Chris hopes to flip the house to Emma for $105,000. Unless Emma is very foolish, she is not going to pay Chris $105,000 if Brian can force her to sell the house back to him for $85,000. See Appendix C for information on redemptory rights in each state.

What sort of Plan B should a flipper have in case the market takes a downturn?

Flippers need to be very sensitive to trends in their local market. If housing prices are edging downward, and if foreclosures are on the upturn, the market might become flooded with properties. Lenders are not in the real estate business. They are just not set up to manage, insure, maintain, and market homes. In a flooded market, they will begin slashing prices just to move inventory. That is your competition if you are a flipper. You will be competing against lenders trying to dispose of foreclosed homes and other flippers able to purchase more cheaply than you did.

If your housing market fits this profile, you will need to buy more cheaply than you perhaps originally anticipated. That is so you will have a larger cushion in case you face heavy price competition when you are ready to sell.

You should also be prepared to hold the house longer than antic-ipated, renting it out to cover your holding expenses. Make sure you have properly evaluated the rental opportunities for any house you want to buy. When preparing a budget for that possibility, be sure to include mortgage payments, insurance, real estate taxes, homeowners' association dues, and reasonably anticipated expenses. Finally, have a lender lined up for long-term financing for several years. Most flippers borrow money for short terms of six to twelve months. Unless you have a commitment to renew your loan several times, or you have a take-out lender for permanent financing, you could find yourself facing foreclosure.

If my goal is to build a portfolio of rental properties, do foreclosures present any special opportunities?

Many so-called foreclosure experts tell you to *never* rent a property to the former owner. I disagree. In fact, I encourage you to seek out opportunities that will allow you to rent to the former owner.

Tenants, as a group, come in all degrees of financial responsibility, and a broad spectrum of good or bad property caretakers. You have to evaluate each one, and you can take nothing for granted. It is the same with former owners of foreclosed real estate.

Remember, many former owners were not irresponsible. They just found themselves in a financial bind they could not work their way out of. Often, it was the accumulated past due payments after a short-term money problem that was their downfall. They could have made the monthly payments on the home, but they could not catch up on the arrearages.

You might wonder why the former owner did not talk to his or her lender and work out a payment plan for the arrearages, or why he or she did not file for Chapter 13 bankruptcy. The answer is usually fairly simple. Most people do not know their lender will work with them. They become scared, do not return phone calls, and do not even open mail from their lender. They are headed for a train wreck called foreclosure, with no clue how to stop it. Many will avoid bankruptcy because of the stigma, the invasion of privacy, or they believe (correctly) that a foreclosure will drop off their credit record before a bankruptcy does.

In my experience, former owners make long-term, stable tenants who take good care of the property. They are already emotionally invested in it, and they consider it their home, not a rental house. Especially if they have children, they are very motivated to keep as much as possible normal in their lives, despite recent financial turmoil. Obviously, this strategy will not work for postforeclosure purchases because the former owners have already moved on.

Other than former owners as tenants and the opportunity to buy at less than full market value, foreclosures do not have any special considerations for rental income investors.

How do I invest in redemptory rights?

Some states give foreclosed owners the right to buy their property back at the foreclosure bid price. They have different time periods depending on the state, ranging from three months to twelve months.

Buying *rights of redemption* is similar to buying options on real estate. You pay the former owner a small sum of money, usually $500 to $1,000. You receive a deed or a bill of sale (depending on the state) for the redemptory rights. That gives you the right to buy the property for the foreclosure bid price at any time before the redemptory period expires.

This type of investing is only for the very experienced. It requires you to know every nook and cranny of a subtle area of law. The person who sold you the right of redemption might not be the only one entitled to redeem the property. If you purchase the property, someone else might be able to then buy it from you for the same price. While you will get your purchase price back if this happens, you will not be reimbursed for the interest on the money you borrowed to finance the purchase, the money you spent on the closing, or any other prepurchase expenses such as home inspections.

Another type of redemption investing is to buy at foreclosure, usually real estate tax sale foreclosures. You buy at a very low price, secure in the knowledge that the former owner will be able to redeem at some point in the future. Tax sales often carry much longer redemption periods than regular foreclosures, sometimes as long as three years.

Why are you hoping the former owner redeems in such situations? Suppose you have some money to invest. You can put it in CDs at the bank, for very low interest rates. Or, you can put it in the stock market and hope you choose the right stocks. Or, you can buy tax sale and similar properties because most states require the redeeming owner to pay 12% interest. They must reimburse you for your purchase price, plus 12% per year in interest, plus (usually) money you spent for taxes and insurance. If you buy right, the worst thing that happens is that the former owner never redeems and you have a valuable piece of real estate for a very small investment.

Some people recommend reselling to the former owner rather than renting to the former owner. How is that done?

The former owner will not be able to borrow the money to repurchase his or her home right away. The only way this strategy works is if you are the lender for the former owner. This is usually accomplished through something called a *bond for title, contract for deed,* or *land sale contract.* They are all pretty much the same arrangement.

The former owner, as the purchaser, pays a modest down payment of around 5% of the value of the property. He or she then makes monthly rental payments higher than market rates. If he or she makes all the monthly payments on time, the seller gives him or her a deed at the end. If the buyer misses a payment, he or she is evicted. There is no time-consuming foreclosure. Bankruptcy laws often cannot cure the default and preserve any equity in the property.

As generally practiced, this is a very predatory and heavy-handed way of selling properties. I know someone who pursues this strategy because, as he says, "Most buyers will default in the first six months, forfeiting their down payment." He makes a tidy profit on forfeited down payments. He says that he at least gives former owners a fighting chance, which is more than their lenders were willing to do. Some former owners actually pull it off, recover from their financial setbacks, and are able to obtain regular mortgage money to buy out of the bond for title. Most do not, though.

Many states severely limit the practice. Others give consumers rights similar to those held by mortgage borrowers. Before heading down this road, make sure you know your state's consumer protection laws in this area.

Chapter 4

FINDING APPROPRIATE PROPERTIES

- How much cash do I need?
- What borrowing resources do I need?
- How can I borrow more than the purchase price to buy real estate?
- How good are foreclosure websites?
- What are some of the better websites?
- How do I find preforeclosures?
- How do I find foreclosure auctions?
- Can I really buy government-owned real estate for $1?
- How do I find real estate owned by the U.S. government?
- How do I find real estate owned by state and local governments?
- Are there any restrictions on buying from the government?
- What is the best way to use scouts?
- I want homeowners in distress to find me. Is that possible?
- Can I become a preferred buyer for real estate lenders, so they will call me first?
- You have given me a lot of resources for foreclosures. How do I sift through all the information?

How much cash do I need?

In some circumstances, preforeclosure buyers may be able to simply take over the monthly mortgage payments and have a workable plan for catching up with past due amounts. Especially in a time of increasing foreclosure rates, lenders are very motivated to avoid adding to the inventory. They might be willing to forgive some past due interest, reverse late charges, and split the difference on legal fees and other expenses. If they would do this with you, why would they not do it with the borrower? Because the borrower is probably too frightened and emotional to talk to the lender, and because the borrower is now tainted in the lender's mind. The lender needs a fresh face—someone with a good credit score—to take over the payments. That could be you.

Auction buyers will have to check with the attorney or trustee in charge of the sale. Sometimes bidders must register by depositing earnest money with the auctioneer in order to show the financial ability to proceed to closing. Other times you must pay a certain percentage, from 5% to 20% on the day of the closing, with the balance due in thirty to sixty days. The requirements vary among states, lenders, and auctioneers.

Postforeclosure cash requirements are very much like buying any other real estate. As I write this book, there is a lot of worry in Washington, D.C., and on Wall Street about increasing numbers of foreclosures and their impact on the economy. One aspect of the problem is the issue of lenders and investors holding large inventories of foreclosed real estate. I predict that these groups will become much more motivated to engage in creative solutions, including holding 100% of the financing for sales of foreclosed real estate. Regulatory and accounting barriers that currently make this very difficult may have already been removed by the time this book reaches your hands.

Always ask if the owner of foreclosed real estate will finance your purchase for 100% of the purchase price and waive all closing costs. Be prepared to pay a higher purchase price than if you had cash.

For other types of foreclosure-like sales, such as tax auctions, creditor sales, or bankruptcy sales, you should ask whoever is conducting the sale about his or her cash requirements. These can vary widely.

What borrowing resources do I need?

There are three general sources of financing available to purchase foreclosure properties. If your goal is to buy a home for yourself, the typical mortgage loan sources are always available to you. Investors and flippers can usually borrow money on a short-term basis for more than 100% of the purchase price *if they have a credible plan for repairing or rehabbing the property and increasing its value.* I will address that in the next question.

Foreclosing lenders or servicing companies may be able to provide financing to you by allowing assumption of the defaulted loan. Even postforeclosure properties can sometimes be purchased with seller financing. Always ask about this option if it is important to you.

Many foreclosure advice experts tell you to obtain a line of credit at a bank for your purchase, which often is more easily said than done. If you have substantial equity in your home, you can obtain a home equity line of credit. If you have excellent credit, substantial liquid assets (stocks, bonds, or cash), and a great investing reputation in your community, you can probably obtain an unsecured line of credit.

Remember, though, that drawing down a line of credit is a short-term solution. Interest rates are usually relatively high, and the line of credit must generally be renewed each year. Lenders become nervous if you have maxed out your line of credit and do not reduce it after a year or so. When lenders are nervous, you pay, through higher interest rates, increasing rollover fees, and demands that you provide collateral for your line of credit.

The HUD Good Neighbor Next Door program provides an excellent opportunity for 100% financing. For details, see the answer to "Are there specialized programs for homeowners to buy foreclosed properties?" in Chapter 3.

Buying at tax sales usually requires no access to borrowed funds. The tax bills are generally relatively small and can be paid from cash resources. You may need a line of credit if you plan to buy many tax sale properties in the expectation that former owners will redeem within a short period of time and pay you 12% interest on your money. A strategy of targeting one or two tax sale properties in the hopes of being able to keep the real estate, however, should not require borrowed funds.

How can I borrow more than the purchase price to buy real estate?

For normal home purchases, in order to buy a house for $100,000, you will have to come up with $20,000 as a down payment if you have conventional financing (no FHA insurance or VA guarantee) and no private mortgage insurance (PMI). That is because of requirements made by the investors who buy home mortgages after they are originated.

Commercial loans are entirely different. Borrowers with good credit and good reputations in the community can borrow 100% or more of the purchase price for rental houses, so long as the debt service coverage ratio (DSCR) is 1.2 or better—in other words, if your annual cash flow is 20% more than your annual mortgage payments. Lenders like to know that your property income is enough to make the mortgage payments, even if you have some unusual expenses or greater than ordinary vacancies. To calculate this, use the following worksheet:

Total annual rental income: _____
Minus 5% for vacancies: − _____
Minus insurance: − _____
Minus real estate taxes: − _____
Minus annual repairs/maintenance: − _____
Minus advertising/commissions: − _____
Equals net operating income (NOI)   = _____

Start with NOI _____
Divide by annual mortgage payments ÷ _____
Equals DSCR   = _____

The other way to obtain 100% financing, and sometimes even more, is to have a believable plan to rehab or repair the property and increase its value. This depends on giving your lender a detailed budget for rehab and repair expenses, a timeline for completing them and selling the house or obtaining permanent financing, and the estimated value of the home after the repairs. You must support your estimated value by providing an appraisal, or by supplying your lender with information about recent sales of properties comparable to your own, after the house is completed.

How good are foreclosure websites?

Foreclosure websites are populated with properties listed by participating lenders and real estate brokers. Some of the information is very timely and some is outdated. You should not rely exclusively on websites because of the following reasons.

- Many more properties may be available. Not everything is listed on the websites. The properties featured on the websites will have the most competition because many people use them exclusively.

- Most of the sites charge a membership fee. If you know your target market area, you can usually obtain the same information for free from local sources.

What are some of the better websites?

I do not want to provide an endorsement for any particular service. They all have their strengths and their weaknesses. Some are better in some markets than they are in others.

Do an Internet search on the phrase "foreclosure sales." Include the quotation marks. That will provide you with a number of information services. Bookmark about five or six of them that allow free limited previews of available properties.

Next, check your local home sales magazine for anything with the word *foreclosure* plastered across the ad. Find two or three real estate brokers with foreclosure listings. Call them for details, including how long they have had the listings. Ask if they have any more foreclosure properties besides the one you called about. Make notes regarding all information given to you.

Next, go to the website of Ocwen Financial Corporation at **www.ocwen.com**. It handles the VA foreclosures nationwide. Check for foreclosed homes in your target area. Make a list of the homes available. Call to see if the foreclosed homes are still on the market, what the list prices are, and how long they have been listed. Do the same thing for HUD-owned homes by going to its website,

www.hud.gov, and clicking on the links for "HUD homes" and then the link for your particular state. Call about any listed homes, again noting their availability, their list price, and their time on the market.

Here is the test. Compare the sample information you have gathered against what is available on the foreclosure information websites. Which provider seems to have the most complete, accurate, and up-to-date information? That provider will probably be the best one for your market area.

How do I find preforeclosures?

Finding preforeclosures depends on whether your state uses the *judicial foreclosure method* or the *nonjudicial foreclosure method*. For the most part, states that use deeds of trust have nonjudicial foreclosures. States that use mortgages have judicial foreclosures. Alabama is a hybrid state that uses mortgages with power of sale clauses, allowing nonjudicial foreclosures. A judicial foreclosure requires the filing of a lawsuit before the auction can occur. Nonjudicial foreclosure states do not have that requirement.

In *judicial foreclosure* states, the first public step leading up to foreclosure is filing a *lis pendens* notice. The *lis pendens* is a paper filed in the real estate records for the county or parish where the property is located. It puts the world on notice that there is a pending lawsuit that may ultimately affect the ownership of real estate. Lis pendens notices are not limited to foreclosures, but are used generically in all states whenever there is a dispute over title to real estate and a resulting lawsuit.

In *nonjudicial foreclosure* states, the first step toward foreclosure is often the appointment of a substitute trustee. The trustee is the person authorized in the loan documents to perform the foreclosure auction. Lenders getting ready to foreclose must make sure the proper party has been named as trustee. Usually, this means filing an *Appointment of Substitute Trustee*. It is an early warning sign of impending foreclosure. You can often search online for those documents, or search in person at the offices where deeds are recorded for your community. Call your local recorder of deeds for more information,

You should also read the legal section of your local newspaper or a specialized legal newspaper in your community. Public notices regarding scheduled foreclosures will be printed by the creditors' attorneys. This may only give you a two- to three-week lead, or you may have more time if the foreclosure is postponed several times.

Pending sales of property for delinquent real estate taxes can be obtained from the local tax collector's office. If you do not know where your local tax collector's office is, call any mortgage company or closing company and ask them. Someone there will be able to tell you.

Judgment creditor auctions are usually advertised in the legal section of the newspaper.

How do I find foreclosure auctions?

You find auctions by closely following the legal notices in your local newspaper. By the time of the public notice, however, you generally have only a few weeks to check out the property and any potential title problems. I suggest you start identifying properties at the preforeclosure stage, even if you have no intention of buying before the auction. This will give you the necessary time to do your home-work and be prepared. While a significant percentage of the proper-ties will successfully avoid actual foreclosure, it is better to take time to be prepared and then be disappointed than to make a big mistake because you had insufficient time to fully evaluate an opportunity.

Can I really buy government-owned real estate for $1?

Maybe someone, at some point in time, has been able to buy a piece of real estate for $1, but I would not count on being able to dupli-cate that success. I once represented a seller who owned real estate on which a dry cleaner had operated for many decades. It was a toxic waste site, no doubt about it. He was quite elderly and would have sold the property to anyone for $1. That was because he needed to get the property out of his name before he died and the land ended up in the children's names. If that had happened, they might have been responsible for the cost of the cleanup. As luck would have it, we sold the land to an investor for $100,000, even after full disclo-sure of the hazardous waste.

So, beware of $1 properties. There might be more than meets the eye.

How do I find real estate owned by the U.S. government?

To find government REOs (*real estate owned*, which is shorthand for foreclosure properties), I like to begin with the United States General Services Administration website, **www.govsales.gov**. It provides links to all federal government-owned property for sale, including foreclosures. Agencies include:

- Housing and Urban Development (HUD);

- Veterans Administration (VA);

- U.S. Department of Agriculture (USDA);

- U.S. Marshal's Service (criminal seizures);

- Internal Revenue Service (IRS);

- Small Business Administration (SBA) (which includes rental houses purchased as part of a small business and homes that were given as additional collateral for small business loans); and,

- miscellaneous other agencies that come into possession of real estate.

While shopping at this site for bargains, do not limit yourself to foreclosures. The federal government sells a wide variety of real estate for a multitude of reasons. Many properties can be purchased at bargain prices.

How do I find real estate owned by state and local governments?

State and local governments may become owners of real estate either as a result of low-income housing assistance or unpaid taxes.

Some states have agencies that loan money to qualified citizens to purchase homes. If those borrowers default, the agency will foreclose on their home. To identify any such agencies in your state, call your local HUD office. They maintain a wealth of information about local homeowner assistance programs and will be able to direct you to the proper state agencies.

Unpaid state income taxes can result in property seizure and sales, just like with the IRS. If your state has income taxes, contact the revenue department's enforcement division, usually located in your state capital. They can tell you if anything is currently for sale, identify who handles the sales, and provide you with any resources you can use to keep track of upcoming auctions.

Sales of property to pay for delinquent real estate taxes are another possibility. Call the local office that handles the receipt of such tax payments. It might be called the tax assessor's office, the tax collector's office, or the revenue department. Every state is different. Find out everything you can about the procedures leading up to the tax sales, requirements for bidding at the auctions, and any rights the former owners have after the auction. The latter information will be important to you if you buy property from the state after a tax sale auction.

Many times, there will be no bidders at a sale for unpaid real estate taxes. The state or local authority will bid the property in, and will be the owner, just like a bank that has foreclosed. Usually, a different agency handles the real estate after it has been bid in by the government. Find out what that agency is and who you can contact to see what is in inventory. To discover the responsible authority, call your local tax collector's office.

Are there any restrictions on buying from the government?

I am unaware of any general restrictions on buying real estate from the government. The only one I can think of might have to do with past due child support obligations or unpaid income taxes. I can envision a situation in which someone with such obligations attempts to buy from the government, proceeds to closing, and then his or her earnest money is confiscated for the unpaid sums. You might want to think twice about buying property from the government if you owe child support or taxes.

That being said, national and local governments do give preferences to buyers who intend to live in the properties they purchase. Often, REOs will be offered first to potential homeowners for a specified period of time. If the house has not sold by the expiration of that time, anyone is eligible to make an offer.

What is the best way to use scouts?

Scouts find properties for you in return for a fee if you proceed to closing. The fee is usually small—$500 to $1,000—depending on the value of the property you acquire. The use of scouts multiplies your efforts because you have many people researching all the many sources for foreclosure properties. They often run across preforeclosure opportunities by word-of-mouth. This information lets you get to the borrower long before anyone else and possibly work out a deal that works to the advantage of both of you.

Unfortunately, many states require scouts to have a real estate license. Because of laws recommended by the National Association of Realtors® and by state trade associations and licensing commissions, legislatures around the country passed laws making the use of scouts illegal. The law usually says that only licensed real estate professionals may accept a fee or other compensation for assisting people in finding real estate to buy or lease, which is basically what a scout does.

Some jurisdictions specifically exempt scouts from this very broad language. To find out the law in your state, call your state's real estate licensing authority and ask him or her. Contact information is in Appendix C.

That issue aside, the best way to use scouts is to have a written agreement with each one. There are two problems you want to avoid.

1. What happens if multiple scouts send you information on the same property? How do you determine which one will be paid, and how do you avoid angering the other ones and getting sued?

2. What happens if you find a property by yourself, and then a scout also sends you information on the same house?

Your agreement should have a mechanism for *registering* proper-ties in order to determine who finds property first. I recommend requiring an email message, with the date and time of receipt being the determinant. For your own property finds, send an email to your-self with the information. That way there will always be a record of who knew what and when they knew it.

I want homeowners in distress to find me. Is that possible?

There are many methods of advertising your services so that home-owners facing foreclosure seek you out, rather than the other way around. The most popular way of advertising seems to be those little signs you see everywhere that read, "Facing foreclosure? We buy houses," or something similar.

I have never used that approach but have my doubts about its effectiveness. To research the subject, I have called many of the listed telephone numbers on the signs. I always end up talking to someone in a call center. Apparently the signs work only if you sift through large numbers of phone calls from homeowners with unsuitable properties or who call too late for a deal. Somewhere in there is a nugget or two of gold. You, personally, cannot screen that many phone calls, so you will have to hire a service. These services charge by the call—good prospects, bad prospects, and calls from the merely curious. The economics may or may not work for you.

In another one of my books, I recommend speaking to groups about foreclosure options. Many of the people in your audience will learn enough to avoid foreclosure. That is a good thing. If there are too many foreclosures, it will only depress the price of your own purchases. You want the inventory large enough to support your purchases, but not so large that real estate prices take a nose dive. The attendees who cannot or will not solve their own problems will need someone to help them with a preforeclosure purchase. They will come to you.

Even if you cannot help someone through buying his or her home before the foreclosure, you do gain advance knowledge of the upcoming auction. Unlike other auction buyers, you will have already met the borrower, inspected the property, and been able to prepare a realistic budget. You may feel comfortable placing the former owner in the house as a tenant, or you may know better. The point is that you have far more knowledge than other auction bidders. That gives you a distinct advantage.

Can I become a preferred buyer for real estate lenders, so they will call me first?

Because of privacy laws, lenders are not allowed to call you when a loan goes into default or might be foreclosed. The best you can expect is that a lender might give your card to a borrower in trouble, as someone who might help. This is certainly a good strategy, and you should pursue it with local real estate lenders.

After foreclosure, lenders and servicing companies generally rely on real estate agents to market their properties. Learn which companies in town are the preferred brokers for foreclosure properties. Get to know the agents. Once you establish your credibility as a serious buyer, ask them to notify you as soon as something new comes into their inventory. This gives you a head start before the other buyers see the ads. It also saves the agent some advertising and marketing money if you buy before those expenses are incurred.

You have given me a lot of resources for foreclosures. How do I sift through all the information?

You should do the following.

- Identify what you want in an ideal property as far as location and features.

- Pick out your area of focus—preforeclosure, auction, or post-foreclosure.

- If you plan to rent out a property, target a rental range that your property should command from the marketplace.

- If you are a flipper, pick a price range for the sales price after the flip and a budget range for rehab and repair expenses.
- If you are a homeowner, pick a price range with monthly payments you can comfortably afford. Beware of mansions at bargain foreclosure prices. Your mortgage payment may be affordable, but the ongoing maintenance, repairs, taxes, and insurance could bankrupt you.

- Set a budget for your purchase price. This is next to last on the list because you will normally have to do a good bit of research and possibly even negotiating before arriving at your purchase price. Reject properties that are unacceptable for other reasons before you get down to examining possible purchase prices.

- Set a budget for how much time you will spend on this project. By this I mean how many hours each and every weekday and how many hours on the weekend. If you rely on your spare time to research properties, the information will just pile up on you. You will become discouraged, and nothing will happen. You will never buy a thing.

Chapter 5

UNDERSTANDING THE PARTIES AND THEIR MOTIVATIONS

- Who are the various parties in a foreclosure?
- Why do I need to know all the parties who might be involved in a foreclosure?
- What motivates the owner?
- How does knowing owner motivation help me negotiate?
- What motivates the lender?
- How does knowing lender motivation help me negotiate?
- What motivates the servicing company?
- How does knowing servicer motivation help me negotiate?
- What motivates the mortgage insurance company?
- How does knowing PMI motivation help me negotiate?
- What motivates other lienholders in a foreclosure?
- How does knowing other lienholder motivation help me negotiate?
- What motivates other types of creditors besides those with mortgage loans?

Who are the various parties in a foreclosure?

The following is a list of the most common players involved in a foreclosure.

- The *borrower* may also be called a *mortgagor* or a *trustor*, depending on your state.

- The *lender* may also be called a *mortgagee* or the *beneficiary*, depending on your state.

- The *trustee* is the person appointed under a deed of trust to hold legal title to the real estate. The trustee may sell the property after a default. In the alternative, the trustee must transfer title to the borrower after all the loan payments have been made.

- The *servicing company* collects mortgage payments, makes sure taxes and insurance payments are made under budget mortgages, interacts with the borrower, and distributes mortgage payments to various investors according to its instructions.

- *Mortgage Electronic Registration System* (MERS) acts as the nominee for mortgage loan owners. In that way, the loan can be sold several times without constantly having to update real estate records with the names of the new owners.

- The *Federal Housing Administration* (FHA) insures mortgages that meet its underwriting guidelines. If the borrower defaults, the FHA will either pay off a claim to the lender or it will buy the mortgage loan and proceed with foreclosure.

- The *Veterans Administration* (VA) guarantees mortgages for borrowers who meet its eligibility requirements. If the borrower defaults, the VA will either pay off the claim to the lender, or it will buy the mortgage loan and proceed with foreclosure.

- Mortgage Guaranty Insurance Corporation is the largest and oldest of the *private mortgage insurance* (PMI) companies. It performs the same function as the FHA, except for loans that do not meet the FHA requirements.

- *Investment trust* is an entity that may own many millions of dollars of mortgage loans it purchased on the secondary market. The investment trust usually issues bonds that are backed by those mortgages. Bond purchasers can be individuals, retirement plans, insurance companies, large investment firms, and even banks and mortgage companies.

- The *Financial Accounting Standards Board* establishes accounting rules that impact the amount of discretion servicing companies have when dealing with defaulted loans or loans that might go into default.

- The *Internal Revenue Service* (IRS) is charged with collecting the nation's taxes. It seizes real estate when those taxes are not paid. The IRS also takes the position that debt forgiveness is the same thing as income and is therefore taxable. Foreclosure investors who are able to buy properties at discounts from lenders before foreclosure usually also obtain debt forgiveness for the borrower. As a result, the borrower might owe additional income taxes. There is a move to change this law because of its oppressive consequences.

- The *real estate broker* is the licensed professional who is supposed to market foreclosed real estate for the owner, handle negotiations within the limits of his or her authority and seek additional authority when warranted, and secure the highest price on the best terms for the property.

- *Lienholders* are other parties who have claims against the property as a result of some sort of debt or court order. Liens can arise as a result of other mortgages, unpaid taxes, unpaid condo or subdivision dues and assessments, court judgments by creditors, liens by repair persons, divorce orders, and a wide variety of other methods. With the exception of real estate taxes and the liens by repairpersons, liens must be recorded in the real estate records to be effective.

Why do I need to know all the parties who might be involved in a foreclosure?

When you buy real estate in a normal transaction, you negotiate directly with the owner or the owner's real estate agent. You rarely come into contact with anyone else, and you certainly do not need to craft any solutions to meet the needs of multiple parties. All of that is different when you buy foreclosures.

You might think you can simply call the lender named in the mortgage or deed of trust and work out a deal. When clerical personnel seem to be giving you the runaround, you might become discouraged and quit. If you understand all the parties involved, you may be better informed than the person on the other end of the phone. You can ask direct and pointed questions to find the person with the required authority to talk to you.

Often, you will be able to talk to only one of the parties, but you still have to consider the needs of the other parties. More than likely, one or more of the parties will have to accept less than everything on their wish list. Knowing the parties and their motivations can help you come up with a workable solution and persuasively argue why your solution is better than the alternatives.

The least sophisticated party in the whole mix will probably be the borrower. Add to that the fact that the borrower is emotionally involved and probably not able to think things through in a fully rational manner. If you are negotiating with borrowers, you will need to educate them on their options and explain why your solution will produce a good outcome for them. You cannot rely on a borrower to understand the big picture when you offer something. It is a difficult time for him or her, and you must be explicit.

What motivates the owner?

In a perfect world, preforeclosure owners want to avoid the stigma of foreclosure, get the lender off their back, have a little money in their pocket, and retain a chance to preserve some semblance of their standard of living. Buyers who can craft a solution that meets as many of these needs as possible have a higher probability of success in their purchases. Borrowers facing foreclosure are generally reconciled to the idea that they will lose ownership of their home.

How does knowing owner motivation help me negotiate?

Let us look at each of the owner's goals in turn and see how you can meet them.

- Avoiding the stigma of foreclosure can easily be accomplished through a preforeclosure purchase.

- Getting the lender off the owner's back can happen in one of two ways. If your state is a nondeficiency judgment state, this happens automatically. If not, you can negotiate for the lender to forgive any remaining balance on the debt. The lender will never see that money anyway. For the time being, the borrower will probably be judgment-proof. The lender will sell the deficiency claim to someone else for a penny or two on the dollar. The lender would much rather give up that claim if it will help him or her sell the property to a qualified buyer. See Chapter 8 for additional details on this issue.

- To help the owner have a little money in his or her pocket, buyers in states with postforeclosure rights of redemption can offer to purchase those rights from the borrower. This speeds up the ability to sell the property. You can defer payment until you actually flip the property, or until you place permanent financing on it if you plan to be a landlord or a homeowner. In all states, you can offer to make the former owner a silent partner who will share a small percentage of your profits, comparable to what you would pay a scout.

- The former owner can retain his or her standard of living if you are willing and able to rent to him or her. His or her life can continue as if he or she never faced foreclosure; he or she does not have to move, the neighbors do not gossip, and the children do not have to change schools. These are all huge motivators.

What motivates the lender?

First, we are using the term *lender* generically in this case to mean the owner of the promissory note secured by the real estate in danger of foreclosure. It might not actually be the original lender. In fact, it will rarely be the original lender. Second, this particular section applies only to mortgage lenders, not to the other types of creditors such as the IRS, judgment creditors, real estate tax collectors, and so on. Those will be covered in the answer to another question later on in this chapter.

So, what does motivate the lender? In a perfect world, the lender would continue to receive the income stream he or she anticipated over the period of time he or she expected to earn income. Receiving a lump sum of cash is certainly better than taking title to real estate through foreclosure, which is itself better than nothing. On the other hand, if those lenders want to loan money out and receive it back in a relatively short amount of time, they would make short-term loans, not home mortgage loans.

To further muddy the waters, many home mortgages were sold on the secondary market and then repackaged as bonds with differing maturities and interest rates. The whole system depends on borrowers making their payments according to pre-established schedules. Yes, the models do anticipate that some loans will default and others will be paid off early through home sales or refinancing. Large numbers of defaults throw a monkey wrench in the calculations, though.

Remember, the primary motivation is to continue receiving a stream of income. The secondary motivation is to minimize losses. The second goal might be met easily if there is PMI coverage, which shifts the lender's loss to a third party. You might hit a brick wall with lender negotiations and wonder why the lender does not seem more motivated to reach a solution that will ultimately return more money to him or her than other options. The answer might be that the other options might not result in as much of a loss as you think because of the existence of PMI coverage.

How does knowing lender motivation help me negotiate?

If preservation of the income stream is a primary goal, then a buyer who wishes to assume the defaulted loan should be very attractive to a lender. The first question you should ask all lenders is, "Subject to underwriting conditions to make sure I am creditworthy, is it possible to assume the loan?"

Unfortunately, many lenders will tell you that assumption is not possible. That may be because it is not allowed under their various contracts with other parties. It might be that assumption is not allowed at that particular stage of default. For example, the people in customer service who deal with current loans or those less than 60 days past due may not know anything about loan assumptions. At that stage, it might not be allowed. But, if the loan becomes 60, 90, or 120 days past due, there may be different rules.

If you are not happy with the answer you receive, always ask for a second opinion from a supervisor. Also, be sure to ask the supervisor if there will be different rules at a later stage in the default.

What motivates the servicing company?

The servicing company earns money by efficiently servicing loans, preferably by continuing to service the ones already in its portfolio. Foreclosures are not good for the company, nor is it good for a buyer to pay off the defaulted loan and obtain financing elsewhere. It would be in the servicing company's best interest if you would assume the loan, continue making payments, and it could continue earning its fees. In that regard, servicing companies have the same motivation as lenders.

Unfortunately, servicing companies have very lengthy and compli-cated contracts spelling out their rights, authority, and obligations. As much as their personnel might want to acquire you as a customer with an assumption and retain the defaulted loan, their hands might be tied.

Keep in mind, also, that servicing companies must work very efficiently if they are to make a profit. You are only one of the very many foreclosure investors with whom they will come in contact. If there are as few as one hundred of you—an unrealistically small number for large servicers—they cannot afford to spend time on creative solutions. The legal department will have to render an opinion regarding whether assumption of the loan is allowed or not. The loan owner will have to give his or her consent, if that is required. The company's legal department will have to determine if it is allowed to give consent or if its structure and stakeholders make that impossible. All this might be insurmountable for you.

How does knowing servicer motivation help me negotiate?

Remember the efficiency motivation when talking to servicing companies. Be prepared. Have all supporting documentation available. If you argue in favor of a lower value than the price demanded, have complete information about comparable sales. The servicer will have to make a case to superiors supporting the acceptance of a lower price or a less than complete payoff. I usually like to make it easy for them to plagiarize my material. The more documentation I give a servicer, the better my chances of getting what I want.

Put everything in writing, so a new person assigned to the file can get up to speed quickly. Reference the servicer's file number on all correspondence so employees do not waste time trying to find the loan you are writing about. Begin all letters and emails with a short recap of recent events. If you refer to a document already submitted to the servicer, attach another copy of the letter that references the document. That way, no one has to find the prior correspondence or documents. Remember, these are very busy people with massive internal pressure to maximize returns by spending as little time as possible on each loan. Help them, and in doing so you will help yourself.

What motivates the mortgage insurance company?

Private mortgage insurance (PMI) companies become involved when a borrower needs a loan larger than 80% of the value of his or her real estate. If neither FHA insurance nor VA guarantees are available, PMI comes into play. The PMI companies write policies that protect lenders from the consequences of loaning more than 80% of the value of a home by insuring a portion of the loan. They must pay off the lender if the loan goes to foreclosure and brings an insufficient amount of money to pay off the loan.

If the lender bids on the property, the PMI company reduces the lender's claim by the amount of the bid, plus any profit made when the lender sells the foreclosed real estate.

Usually, the lender must notify the PMI company when a loan is between 60 and 120 days past due. At that time, the PMI company will ask if the lender has procedures in place to counsel the borrower and attempt to preserve the loan. If not, or if the lender contacts have been ignored by the borrower, then the PMI company will request permission to contact the borrower directly.

Because the insurance company will probably have to pay a claim if there is a foreclosure, it is very motivated to avoid that outcome. If foreclosure cannot be prevented, then the PMI company wants to maximize the sales price of the real estate and, as a result, reduce the amount of its insurance payout.

How does knowing PMI motivation help me negotiate?

First, the PMI company may not be your friend in finding a solution. If the current loan can be salvaged by the PMI company counseling the borrower to enter Chapter 13 bankruptcy, the company will do so. That is good for the borrower, the lender, the servicer, and the PMI company, but bad for you.

Not everyone is a Chapter 13 candidate, however. In addition, many Chapter 13 bankruptcies are converted to Chapter 7 liquidations, where the property proceeds to foreclosure. Bankruptcy may only delay the inevitable, while adding to the lender's attorney's fees and other expenses.

Aside from that consideration, remember that for many loans the PMI company will bear the ultimate loss of a foreclosure. Say you want to buy a preforeclosure property worth $120,000 but with an outstanding loan balance of $119,000. The lender might be willing to write the loan down to $96,000 and allow assumption with no money down. In the alternative, the lending company might be willing to accept $96,000 as payment in full for the loan. However, the lender must check with the PMI company first because the PMI company will probably have to write the lender a check for the difference between the value of your offer and the outstanding balance on the loan.

You have those same considerations if you are buying property that has already been foreclosed. The PMI company takes into account the lender's foreclosure bid price, plus the ultimate sales price of the home. Naturally, the PMI company wants the sales price to be as high as possible.

Although PMI companies can and do request permission from servicers to negotiate workouts, they do not always have that opportunity. You will usually be negotiating with the servicer, even though the PMI company and the presence of its insurance is a very important consideration.

I never like to trust someone else to do my negotiating for me. If the person I am talking to must persuade someone else of the wisdom of my plan, I put all my arguments in writing. That way, the person with whom I am talking can simply copy my writing and transmit it to the third-party decision-maker. If you follow the same strategy, especially when it is likely the loan has PMI coverage, you will meet with greater success in your negotiations.

What motivates other lienholders in a foreclosure?

Other lienholders should be separated into two categories: *senior lienholders* and *junior lienholders*. These descriptions are always made relative to the loan being foreclosed. The IRS might be a junior lienholder in relation to a first mortgage being foreclosed, because the IRS lien was filed after the mortgage. On the other hand, that same lien might be a senior lien if the second mortgage is being foreclosed because the lien might have been filed after the first mortgage but before the second mortgage.

Senior lienholders want to receive full payment plus all attorney's fees, accrued interest, and costs of collection. They are in a position of supreme power when a junior mortgage or lien is being foreclosed because the senior lien will remain on the property.

Junior lienholders will almost always receive no money at all after a foreclosure. They might be paid later, even many years later, if the borrower recovers from his or her financial problems. As a result, junior lienholders are motivated to keep the borrower out of bankruptcy so the junior debt will not be obliterated forever.

Some states give junior lienholders the *right to redeem* the property after a foreclosure. Let us assume that Dwight owes 1st National $80,000 on a first mortgage. He also owes 2nd National $10,000 on a second mortgage. Suppose the house is realistically worth $150,000. 1st National forecloses, and you are the only bidder at the auction. You buy the house for $80,100 and receive the title to the real estate free of the 2nd National lien.

Because the house is worth so much more than the combined debts, 2nd National might want to redeem the property if state law allows that. 2nd National might be able to pay you $80,100 and force you to sell the house to it. 2nd National will then be able to sell the house for something close to its true value, recover its redemption price of $80,100, pay off its second mortgage of $10,000, and make a profit. In the real world, this rarely happens, but it is always a possibility.

How does knowing other lienholder motivation help me negotiate?

You will typically not be able to negotiate with senior lienholders. They hold all the power and will have to be paid in full if someone junior to them is foreclosing. You might be tempted to say to yourself, "If the junior lienholder is foreclosing, and the property will still be subject to the senior lien, then it must be worth at least as much as those two debts combined." This would be a mistaken assumption. Never assume someone else knows more than you and never base your decisions on that assumption. If you cannot justify the value from your own research, do not let other parties' possibly foolish decisions sway your opinion.

You generally do not need to negotiate with junior lienholders unless there is substantial equity in the property. In that case, you want to avoid their possible exercise of a right of redemption after foreclosure, and you want to avoid a bidding war at the foreclosure auction. Remember that virtually no lender wants real estate—they want cash.

If you are worried about junior lienholders, remember that they are worried about owning a house. In particular, they are fearful of good money chasing bad, and having to pay off a senior lienholder in order to acquire real estate so they can possibly sell it and then recoup their losses. That is a lot of risk for them. Knowing this, you can negotiate with them to accept less than their full claim.

What motivates other types of creditors besides those with mortgage loans?

- Real estate taxing authorities want past due taxes paid, and they want the real estate returned to private ownership so it can continue to generate taxes in the future. If you are trying to buy property that has been bid on by the government, you may be able to pay less than the full amount of accrued taxes.

- The IRS wants to liquidate real estate as quickly as possible. Speed is more important than maximizing value. IRS auctions usually advertise a minimum bid amount, but that amount can be waived with the taxpayer's permission and IRS management approval. If a sale cannot take place, the IRS will either release the property to the taxpayer and allow the lien to remain until a later date, or it might bid on the property itself. Usually, the IRS prefers not to bid on property. Knowing this, you can negotiate with the owner and the IRS after an unsuccessful auction and persuade everyone to accept less than the full value of the property.

- Bankruptcy trustees must liquidate real estate as quickly as possible, but they generally have legal obligations to maximize value to creditors. Because of this, the trustee must make sure it is immune from criticism that might come after the sale of real estate for possibly insufficient money. Trustees will need to pursue auctions or sealed bids after appropriate advertising and invitations for bids. A private sale usually stands a better chance of court approval if the buyer has an appraisal to support the offered price. *Member Appraisal Institute* (MAI) appraisals have more weight than those prepared by appraisers who do not have the MAI certification.

Chapter 6

READY, SET, BUY!

- How do I estimate the value of real estate?
- What are the steps to estimating value using the comparables method?
- Is there a way to find out the actual sales prices for houses so I can evaluate the comparables?
- I do not have a degree in finance. Can I still capitalize income to arrive at an estimate of value?
- What are the most popular preforeclosure strategies?
- What is the short sale strategy?
- What are the most popular auction strategies?
- What are the most popular postforeclosure strategies?
- Which strategy is the best?
- Do I need a real estate agent?
- Will a real estate agent keep my information confidential?
- Is there any advantage to not having a real estate agent?
- What should I know about real estate contracts in general?
- Must I pay earnest money when I offer to buy property?
- How can I be sure about the property condition?
- What happens if the seller refuses to close?
- Why do real estate contracts describe a certain type of deed?
- If the former owner will remain as a tenant, do I need anything special in the sales contract?
- Must I address seller financing or loan assumption terms in my contract?
- How do I prepare a preforeclosure offer?

How do I estimate the value of real estate?

There are two approaches to estimating the value of most of the properties you will encounter. The *comparables approach* looks at recent sales of comparable properties in order to determine the value of your property. The *capitalized income approach* looks at the income from a rental property and what an investor would pay in order to receive that income stream.

Whatever your ultimate plans for a property, I recommend that you use both approaches, even if they result in different values. Future homeowners or flippers may be competing against investors, and vice versa. Being able to calculate the probable value of a property to a competitor may give you a bidding advantage.

What are the steps to estimating value using the comparables method?

The underlying philosophy of the comparables approach to value is that buyers will pay the same amount of money for roughly similar properties. Minor differences between properties are unimportant. You would look at *comparable properties* and then adjust the sales price of the property you are valuating upward or downward depending on how it compares relative to the properties under consideration.

As an example, let us assume there have been several recent sales of three-bedroom, three-bath brick homes on quarter-acre lots within walking distance of an elementary school in a good school district. They are listed in the following chart, along with the differences between the homes.

Form: Comparable Home Sales Analysis

Date: _____

Comparable 1 address: _____

Comparable 2 address: _____

Comparable 3 address: _____

My property address: _____

Question	1	2	3	Foreclosure
Asking price	$125,000	$110,000	$105,000	_____
Actual sales price	$109,000	$103,000	$101,000	_____
Approximate square feet	1,200	1,100	1,100	1,250
Lot/land size	1/4 acre	1/4 acre	1/4 acre	1/4 acre
Age of house	30	30	30	30
Age of roof	new	10	12	10
Exterior: brick, wood, etc.	Brick	Brick	Brick	Brick
# bedrooms	3	3	3	3
# bathrooms	2	2	2	2
Quality of finishes*	Budget	Budget	Budget	Budget
Garage/carport	Carport	Carport	2-car	2-car
Fenced backyard	Yes	No	Yes	No
Condition	Fair	Excellent	Good	Poor

*"Finishes" are the finishing touches that personalize a home. What is the quality of the carpet, cabinetry, wood trim, doors, counters, wallpaper, lighting fixtures, and plumbing fixtures?

Based on these comps, your foreclosure house is most like the first comparison property, except that your property lacks a fenced-in yard, enjoys a garage instead of a carport, and is in a little worse condition. Depending on the neighborhood, I would probably say that the garage on the foreclosure house is worth a little bit more than the fenced-in yard on the first comparison house, but not a lot. Those two features probably cancel each other out for the purposes of estimating value. That leaves us with the first comparison house selling for $109,000. It was in fair condition, and our house is in poor condition. As a result, the highest value for the foreclosure property is $109,000, and you must discount that for how bad that "poor" condition really is.

Estimating value is that simple. You might have more points of difference, some of which will cause upward adjustments and some of which will cause downward adjustments in the estimate of your home's value. Just do like the professional appraisers, and take each difference in its turn, calculating how much up, and how much down. Then you do the simple arithmetic at the end to arrive at your own estimate of value.

Is there a way to find out the actual sales prices for houses so I can evaluate the comparables?

Real estate agents with access to the full MLS database can generally find out the actual selling prices of property. That is because they share the information with each other via MLS as their properties go to the closing table. If you are working with an agent to find potential flips, he or she can supply you with that information.

Going solo—without an agent—just means you will have to work a little bit harder. If your local government real estate records are online, that is the easiest way to get the information. The officer who records deeds and other real estate instruments will often show the sales price on the face of the document or in the notes. In some places, people who prepare deeds must state the sales price within the body of the deed. Another possibility is to check with the property tax assessor's office—it might have the information you need.

I do not have a degree in finance. Can I still capitalize income to arrive at an estimate of value?

The process sounds scary, but it is actually fairly easy. Conceptually, you want the answer to the following question: How much would someone pay to receive a particular cash flow from a rental property? This calculation requires the use of something called a *capitalization rate*, or *cap rate* as it is usually called.

You can better understand this concept through an example. Suppose you wanted to earn $12,000 per year from an investment. You could buy a bank certificate of deposit (CD) that pays 3% interest, which means you earn $0.03 (3%) per year for every $1 of the CD.

To find out the size of the CD you need to purchase to earn $12,000 per year when interest rates are at 3%, you write out the following:

$$\$\underline{\quad ? \quad} \times 0.03 = \$12,000.$$

The mystery number can be discovered by dividing $12,000 by 0.03. The answer is $400,000. So in order to earn $12,000 a year, you will have to deposit $400,000. Although this terminology is not used in the context of certificates of deposit, we might say that a cash flow of $12,000 per year, at a cap rate of 3%, results in a value of $400,000.

Suppose, instead, you were looking at a piece of rental real estate. The total rent possible each year is $28,000. *Operating expenses*, such as real estate taxes, insurance, maintenance, repairs, advertising, commissions, and office overhead might cost you $16,000 per year. Mortgage payments are not considered operating expenses, so they are not relevant in this calculation. Depreciation deductions on your taxes are also not considered operating expenses, so they are not relevant, either. If you start with $28,000 per year in gross income and subtract $16,000 per year in operating expenses, you are left with $12,000. That is called the *net operating income* (NOI).

What is the value of a piece of rental property with an NOI of $12,000 per year? You must select a cap rate, something that will perform the same function as the interest rate in the previous CD example. Whereas you might invest cash in an FDIC-insured CD and earn only a 3% return, you might desire a better rate on a riskier real estate venture. How much more interest would you want to earn on your investment? The number you choose is called the *cap rate*.

In any community, commercial real estate brokers and mortgage lenders can tell you the prevailing cap rates for various properties at that time. Cap rates change as interest rates change and as market conditions change. They are not carved in rock for all time.

You might find that relatively modest rental houses in fair condition sell on cap rates of 13%. In other words, if an investor were paying cash to buy a rental house, he or she would want the NOI to be 13% of his or her purchase price.

Using the same formula we used to calculate the size of the CD, you would write:

$$\$\underline{\qquad ? \qquad} \times 0.13 = \$12,000.$$

The mystery number can be discovered by dividing $12,000 by 0.13. The answer is $92,307.69. If prevailing cap rates are 13% for similar properties, an investor would probably pay no more than $92,000 or so to acquire a rental house that will give him or her $12,000 per year in cash flow.

What are the most popular preforeclosure strategies?

First and foremost, you will need to identify a number of properties to follow. Many of them will fall out of the pool as borrowers work out their problems, file for bankruptcy, or simply refuse to talk to anyone. Pursuing one property at a time is very likely to result in you becoming discouraged and quitting.

Even if you learn about one particular opportunity with a very motivated owner, you should still investigate alternatives. Otherwise, you will become emotionally invested in trying to buy that one property, and you could make poor decisions.

Learn how to access your local real estate records in order to search for liens on property. You want to be able to easily and cheaply reject properties with too much debt or too many liens. Next, shop the local title insurance companies for the cheapest rates for title commitments. Some properties that make your first cut might still have title problems. You want to minimize how much you will have to spend in order to find out you cannot do a deal.

Know the details of your state's consumer protection laws as they relate to preforeclosure purchases. Borrowers may be able to cancel contracts, or you might have certain disclosure requirements. Fail to follow the requirements, and you could face heavy penalties or even jail. To find out if your state has such laws and to learn the details of them, call the office of the state attorney, or attorney general, for your state. There is usually a toll-free number. Ask for the consumer help desk for a question regarding preforeclosure purchases. The strategy sometimes goes by the derogatory term *equity stripping* because of the number of abuses in the area.

That being said, the most popular strategies are as follows. They are not all mutually exclusive.

- Assume the loan if possible. Ask for a waiver of the *assumption fee* and the *closing costs*. Ask for a deferral of the first payment so you will have a two- or three-month breathing period during which you will not have to worry about making mortgage payments. If the property proceeds to foreclosure and the lender bids on it, he or she will have no income for at least two to six months, anyway.

- If you cannot assume the loan, you will have to obtain third-party financing, and you cannot reasonably expect the same concessions as with an assumption. Ask the foreclosing lender if there is a PMI company, and if the PMI company will add some cash into the deal to make your purchase workable. It will be cheaper than having to pay off an insurance claim after foreclosure.

- Pay the owner nothing for his or her equity, allowing the owner to escape the stigma of foreclosure or bankruptcy.

- Pay the owner a minor amount for his or her equity.

- Pay the owner a small amount in the future for his or her equity, according to a formula based on the profit you actually make on the house.

- Allow the owner to remain as a tenant for some period of time after the purchase.

- Require the owner to completely vacate the house before you will proceed to closing.

- Condition everything on a clean title report and the issuance of title insurance to you. Junior lienholders might be wiped out in a foreclosure, but they will still have claims against the property if you simply purchase the house from the borrower.

- Obtain releases from junior lienholders for little or no money. This depends on convincing them that there is no equity in the property, and that a borrower free of the worries of homeownership might be able to focus on earning money that can pay junior lienholders some or all of their claims.

What is the short sale strategy?

So-called *short sales* consist of persuading a lender to accept less than the full amount of its claim in return for releasing its lien and allowing a sale of the property to you. The borrower might still be responsible to the lender for the shortage. Some states do not allow a foreclosing lender to sue borrowers for deficiencies still due after a foreclosure or a short sale. Check Appendix C for your state's rules. Knowing the rules will help you evaluate the strength of your bargaining position. Borrowers are more willing to go along with such a strategy if they know it will not cost them in the long run.

For lenders, short sales are purely an economic decision. The considerations for them are as follows.

- How long will the loan remain on the books, failing to produce any income, until the lender can foreclose?

- Will a third party buy at the foreclosure auction or will the lender have to bid on the property?

- What is the likelihood that the borrower will file for bankruptcy or fight the foreclosure and seriously delay the lender in getting its money?

- What will it cost the lender in expenses (taxes, insurance, attorney's fees, condo assessments if applicable, etc.) to pursue a strategy of foreclosure?

- If the lender forecloses, how long will it take to market the property and how much can it expect to net after commissions and sale expenses?

- How much will all the above cost in money, time, resources, and lost opportunities to reinvest money if the lender gets paid earlier (through a short sale), rather than later (after a foreclosure)?

- What discount do you assign for the uncertainty of all these concerns? In other words, if the lender thinks it will net $79,000 on a $100,000 loan balance, is it 100% sure of that or only 95% sure? If it is only 95% certain, then the $79,000 should be discounted another 5%, to $75,050. The lender should be willing to short sale the property to you for $75,050.

Short sales might have bad tax consequences for the borrower. These are easily overcome if you know about them in advance and the borrower is prepared. Read Chapter 8 on taxes for more details.

What are the most popular auction strategies?

Auction bidders need to know about any senior lienholders. You might buy a property that is still subject to other mortgages or liens and end up being in foreclosure yourself. Bidders must have the discipline to set a maximum bid price and stick to that decision. In most cases, you must be prepared to present a cashier's check just to bid, have substantial cash earnest money within a very short time afterward, and be prepared to close within thirty days or so.

To repeat the advice given to preforeclosure buyers: learn how to access your local real estate records in order to search for liens on property. You want to be able to easily and cheaply reject properties with too much debt or too many liens. Next, shop the local title insurance companies for the cheapest rates for title commitments. Some properties that make your first cut might still have title problems. You want to minimize how much you will have to spend just to find out you cannot do a deal.

The following are the most popular strategies for successful bidding.

- Attend several auctions conducted by a variety of lenders and auctioneers. You are there for the education, not to bid. Learn the players and how things work. Eavesdrop on investor conversations or openly ask for advice after revealing that you are not a bidder.

- When asking for advice, start with an open-ended question such as, "What advice do you have for a beginner?" Then, keep your mouth shut and listen to the complete answer. Do not try to show off how much you do know, and do not try to steer the conversation to follow up on a comment. When the speaker is finished, ask any follow-up questions. In addition, ask some direct questions such as, "Do you focus on other stages of foreclosure, and can you tell me why?"; "What are your plans for the property—will you rent it out or sell it?"; and "Does this particular lender usually do a lot of foreclosures?"

- Choose a few properties on which to practice. Do everything you would do as if you planned to bid, including estimating value and establishing a minimum bid price. Go to the auction and see how the bidding reflects your own predictions. Follow up afterward to see what ultimately happens to the property, e.g., what price it sells for or what rent it commands.

- If you plan to buy rental properties, have some tenants already lined up. You might know someone in an apartment who would be willing to pay $1,200 per month for a three-bedroom, two-bath home in a good school district. Go out and find such a property, and be ready to move your tenant in immediately. Bear in mind that any such tenant probably has a lease already. Do not pin your hopes on a potential tenant only to find out that he or she must remain in his or her apartment for another seven months after you buy the foreclosure house.

What are the most popular postforeclosure strategies?

Postforeclosure purchases are easier to make than preforeclosure or auction purchases, but there is more competition for the properties. Start by identifying your urgency and the importance of the various features you want. If you desire to purchase a home as soon as possible because you have young children, you will be fairly rigid in your property requirements and may have to pay a higher price as a result. HUD and other government agencies often give prospective homeowners the first opportunities to buy properties. After a certain time period expires, however, anyone can buy. After that point, homeowners will be competing against investors, not just other homeowners.

People looking for flip opportunities can take more time, but they still need to have fairly specific needs in a property profile. Investors looking for rental properties can be very flexible about location and features, as long as the dollars work out. They can afford to shop whatever bargains are available, which are usually the properties that are many months past the foreclosure event.

The following are the most popular strategies for meeting such goals.

- Identify several sources of postforeclosure property sales information, such as websites and local real estate brokers. Follow all local foreclosures for awhile, keeping track of how long they are on the market and how the ultimate sales prices compare to the beginning asking prices. This gives you a good feel for timing and lender flexibility.

- Follow a few foreclosure auctions in which the property is bid on by the lender. How long does it take that property to show up on a website or with a local broker? That will give you a feel for the head start you might enjoy if you can contact lenders right after foreclosures instead of waiting for public sale information. Sometimes, lenders will tell you that once they foreclose, they can do nothing until all the internal paperwork is completed and the property is turned over to a broker. It is good to identify which companies have that policy.

- Focus on any specialized programs for which you might be eligible, such as the HUD Good Neighbor Next Door program. Details are in Appendix B.

Which strategy is the best?

There is no best strategy. Auctions present the most risk but the best opportunities for deep discounts. Preforeclosures involve the most work, relatively minimal risk, and good discounts. Postforeclosures are the safest, require the least work, but also have fewer bargains.

Do I need a real estate agent?

You do not need a real estate agent if you are comfortable buying and selling real estate and negotiating terms on your own. You may be able to hire a buyer's broker to represent you, but unless the property is listed with an agent willing to split his or her fee, you will have to pay your broker. Fees vary, so be sure you have a clear understanding of what you might owe, and under what circumstances. You might be liable if the broker finds exactly what you are looking for and you then decide not to purchase. A buyer's broker must have a written contract with you, so be sure to read all of its terms before signing.

For postforeclosure properties, you can hire a buyer's broker or you can work with any other real estate agent.

Will a real estate agent keep my information confidential?

Absent a written buyer's brokerage agreement with you, an agent will either be a completely neutral party or will represent the seller as an additional broker. Make sure you understand this concept and ask the agent or broker whom they represent. A neutral broker, sometimes called a *transaction broker*, must keep all your information confidential. A seller's agent must disclose all your information to the seller, even if you thought what you told him or her was supposed to be confidential. If you said, "Offer $89,000, but I'd be willing to go up to $110,000 if they play hard ball," then the person working with you, but acting as an additional seller's agent, would have to disclose all of that to the seller. Guess what the seller's counteroffer would be under those circumstances?

Is there any advantage to not having a real estate agent?

One drawback is that a buyer's broker will add expenses to your transaction because you will have to pay him or her.

Otherwise, the question comes up in the context of postforeclosure sales. Usually, the listing agent will have a contract with the owner, in which the owner agrees to pay a commission upon sale. Let us assume that commission is 6% of the sales price.

Most often, the listing agent will not find the buyer. The buyer will generally be working with another agent in town, looking at many different properties listed with many different agents. Whether that agent is a buyer's broker, a transaction broker, or an additional agent of the seller, the listing agent will usually split his or her commission fifty-fifty with that broker. Mentally, the listing agent has already given up 50% of the commission.

If you are working without an agent, you can use this knowledge to your advantage. You can say, "I offer to pay $117,000, contingent on the listing broker accepting only a 3% commission instead of a 6% commission." Accepting the offer would net $113,490 to the lender, not counting closing expenses. To net the same amount after paying a full 6% commission, the lender would have to demand $121,212 from you. Your offer gives the real estate broker the 3% commission he or she would probably have earned anyway. It gives the lender the $113,490 it would net anyway. But it saves you almost $2,400! That is the advantage of working without an agent.

What should I know about real estate contracts in general?

Real estate contracts must almost always be in writing to be enforceable. There is no legal requirement that signatures be notarized. If you are negotiating with one of several owners, or only one spouse in a community property state, it is a good idea to have a personal requirement of notarized signatures. That way it is harder for the other parties to claim that their signatures were forged.

Must I pay earnest money when I offer to buy property?

Earnest money is not necessary to make an enforceable contract. Your promise to buy and the seller's promise to sell are sufficient. Earnest money merely shows that the buyer probably has the financial resources to close. It also often serves as damages in case the buyer defaults.

If a buyer defaults, forfeiture of the earnest money may not be the only consequence. Unless the contract specifically limits the seller's remedies to keeping the earnest money, the seller may also sue the buyer for damages for breach of contract. Make sure you know your risks, and what you have to lose, before entering a contract.

How can I be sure about the property condition?

Except with auction purchases, you should always demand the ability to conduct a property walk-through and a professional property inspection. If the inspection will not take place until after you sign the purchase contract, make sure you reserve the right to cancel the contract if the inspection is unsatisfactory. Many states also have mandatory property condition disclosure laws. Almost any residential real estate broker can supply you with the forms for these disclosures, if they exist in your state.

Foreclosure auctions present a completely different problem. The borrower may not be very cooperative, and the lender may not be able to grant you access for an inspection. Mandatory property condition disclosures may not apply to foreclosing lenders.

You will probably have to be a bit of a detective. Bring someone with you and go visit the house. Notice the condition of the yard. It usually reflects the condition of the interior. Knock on the borrower's front door, and say, "Hi, my name is Jim/Jane, and I have a few questions about the average cost and quality of home repair companies in the community. Do you have a minute to answer a few questions? I am prepared to pay you five dollars for your time." If the borrower slams the door in your face, you at least have seen a short glimpse of the interior of the house, have gotten a whiff of any pet odor problems, and might have seen evidence of packing. This is certainly more than you knew beforehand. In the best case, the borrower invites you in, lets you tour the house, and points out every repair he or she has paid for in the past two years. Do not forget the five dollars. It gets people's attention every time.

What happens if the seller refuses to close?

If a seller refuses to proceed to closing, the buyer can usually bring a court action to force the sale. It is called a *suit for specific performance*. Some states automatically award attorney's fees to the winning party if someone breaches a contract. Other states do not, and say they will award attorney's fees only if the contract makes that provision.

Why do real estate contracts describe a certain type of deed?

A real estate contract will typically specify what type of deed the seller is willing to give you.

There are four types of deeds that may be given.

1. A *general warranty deed* has the effect of the seller promising you that there are no title defects and no other claimants. If there is a problem later, the seller will pay to defend your title and will be liable to you for damages if the title cannot be

defended. You will almost never receive a general warranty deed in a foreclosure purchase.

2. The *special warranty deed* simply promises that the seller has done nothing to cause title problems.

3. A *bargain and sale deed* means the seller thinks he or she might own some interest in property, but he or she is not making any promises about anything.

4. A *quitclaim deed* means the seller probably does not own anything at all, but whatever he or she does own, he or she is willing to sell to you without promises. Some states use quit-claim deeds to also cover the bargain and sale deed situation.

The problems come up when, for example, your contract requires the seller to deliver a special warranty deed and you discover at closing that a prior owner caused title defects. This could happen if you buy from the lender after foreclosure, and the borrower's IRS liens or spousal claims are still in place. You cannot cancel the closing and receive a refund of your earnest money because by agreeing to give you a special warranty deed, the seller did not claim that he or she would give you clear title. As a result, you do not have a legally valid reason for canceling the purchase.

If the former owner will remain as a tenant, do I need anything special in the sales contract?

If your deal includes the former owner remaining as a tenant, the important lease points must be included in the real estate sales contract. For the most part, this would mean the monthly rent, the term of the lease, the amount and due date of any security deposit, and who is responsible for taxes, insurance, lawn care, snow removal, and general repairs and expenses. State law may have consumer protections regarding elements of the lease, including the maximum security deposit amount allowed. Be sure to check out your state laws before proceeding.

Must I address seller financing or loan assumption terms in my contract?

If your negotiation includes assumption of the seller's loan or new financing to be provided by the lender, those important terms must also be included in the sales contract. Important terms would include the amount to be financed, the interest rate, monthly payments, the due date of the entire loan balance, and the types and estimated amounts of any upfront fees and closing costs.

How do I prepare a preforeclosure offer?

Find a good all-purpose real estate sales contract. Almost any real estate agent can give you a copy of the one his or her company uses. You can also look on the Internet for state-specific forms. Usually there is a small fee for downloading the forms from one of these websites.

Beware of forms that claim to be applicable in all jurisdictions. Most states have their own very specific requirements regarding what must be included in a real estate sales contract and the disclosures that must accompany that contract. Pay particular attention to any consumer protection laws related to preforeclosure purchases. A real estate agent form will not include those provisions.

Chapter 7

FINANCING YOUR PURCHASE

- What are the sources of financing for my purchase?
- How important is a good credit score?
- Will I have to pay points to obtain a loan?
- Does it make sense to pay discount points?
- What is APR?
- What are prepayment penalties?
- Why might I want a fully amortizing loan?
- What is a balloon loan?
- What is the difference between an adjustable rate mortgage and a variable rate mortgage?
- How can I protect myself against high interest rates under an ARM?
- Does an ARM payment cap protect me against high payments?
- Can I get a VA loan for my foreclosure purchase?
- Are FHA loans available for foreclosure purchases?
- How can I calculate my monthly payments?

What are the sources of financing for my purchase?

Most mortgage loans come from one of the following sources: banks, mortgage companies, brokers, savings banks, or credit unions. They are called *conventional loans* if you do not have FHA insurance or a VA guarantee.

The expressions *conforming* and *nonconforming* are used to describe whether or not the loans follow guidelines set by Fannie Mae and Freddie Mac (more later on these two corporations.)

The largest single-family loan Fannie Mae will buy is $417,000, with some exceptions for particular geographic areas. The largest loan Freddie Mac will buy is $359,650. Anything larger cannot be bundled into the standard resale packages. This is important to you because you can generally receive cheaper interest rates if you qualify for a Fannie Mae or Freddie Mac resale of your loan. If you are slightly over the top loan limits, you might want to pay a somewhat larger down payment in order to come within the requirements. Larger loans, often called *jumbo loans*, or *nonconforming loans*, are usually kept in the lender's private portfolio or charged higher interest rates and sold to other types of investors. There is nothing derogatory about a nonconforming loan.

Generally you will not deal with mortgage brokers when shopping for a business loan to buy real estate. In other words, if you plan to buy and flip, or buy and turn the real estate into rental property, you should talk to local lenders, not mortgage brokers. Interest rates for business loans are usually higher than those for home loans. The closing costs may be larger, and loan underwriting might take longer. Bear that in mind when making your plans.

How important is a good credit score?

Credit scores are critically important, but a poor score can be improved or overcome by other means.

In the past, buyers with poor credit scores were able to borrow money under programs called *subprime loans*. These buyers usually paid very high up-front fees and higher interest rates. They may have had penalties to pay if they attempted to refinance into something cheaper. Rather than offering them fixed-rate loans, lenders forced such borrowers into adjustable rate mortgages that could result in very high monthly payments.

Because of the heavy focus on the high number of subprime delinquencies and foreclosures, these practices are no longer that common. It is again difficult for people with poor credit scores to borrow money.

You can overcome this hurdle in several different ways. They include the following.

- Be patient and improve your score. Go to the website for the Fair Isaac Corporation, **www.myfico.com**, for advice. You can also call your local HUD office to obtain copies of pamphlets on the subject.

- Obtain a guarantor with good credit. That will cancel out your own poor score.

- If you have a poor credit score but significant *liquid assets* (cash, stocks, or bonds), you can often borrow money despite your score. You might have to give the lender additional collateral in the form of some of your liquid assets.

Will I have to pay points to obtain a loan?

Borrowers typically pay *points* in connection with a mortgage loan. One point is equal to 1% of the loan. A fee of one point on a

$150,000 loan would be $1,500. Many people get confused and think the points are calculated based on the purchase price. They are not—the *loan amount* is the important number.

The money paid for points can be used for a wide variety of things, so it is important to find out the purpose of the points, as well as the amount, when comparing loans. There are two varieties—*origination points* and *discount points*.

Origination points cover closing expenses and fees, including the mortgage broker's profit. Many of the fees covered by origination points are really just disguised additional profit for the lender, and they are completely negotiable.

Discount points are used to *buy down* your interest rate because you are prepaying some of the interest with the discount points. The amount you can reduce your interest rate varies with the type of loan and market conditions at the time. Typically, though, you will have to make mortgage payments for several years before you start saving money because of the buy-down.

Does it make sense to pay discount points?

The answer to that question depends on how long you anticipate keeping the same loan, and how much interest you will save by paying the discount points. At a very simple level, here is how you estimate the answer to the question.

Suppose you want to borrow $100,000 on a 30-year fixed-rate mortgage. You think you can get a 7% interest rate with no discount points, or you can save 0.25% if you pay one point. The one discount point will cost you $1,000.

Monthly payment at 7.00%	$665.30
Monthly payment at 6.75%	$648.60
Monthly savings	$ 16.70

At a savings of $16.70 per month, it will take you 59.88 months, or almost five years, to save enough money to reimburse yourself for the $1,000 paid in points. Will you own the property that long without refinancing? Probably not. If you do not keep that loan in place for five years, you will have lost money by paying the discount points.

What is APR?

APR is short for *annual percentage rate*. It is the effective rate of a loan after taking into consideration certain up-front fees and expenses. The APR will always be higher than the *face rate* of the loan—the figure quoted in advertising and the amount that appears on the face of the promissory note where it says, "I, _____ promise to pay $_____ at _____% interest per year until paid in full..."

Your true APR might be higher, depending on how long you realistically plan to have that same loan in place. This makes more sense with a very simple example that disregards some subtleties of finance but gets the point across.

Suppose on January 1, you borrow $1,000 for one year, at 6% interest, with no payments due until the end of the year. On December 31, you will pay $1,060, which is the full amount of the principal and the interest. It cost you $60 to borrow the money.

What if the lender required you to pay $60 in origination points before it would loan you the money? In that case, you pay $60 on January 1 and another $60 on December 31. It really cost you $120 to borrow that money. As a practical matter, your true interest rate was 12%, not 6%. That is the essence of the APR calculations.

Now, this is where it starts to get tricky. What if you paid that

$60 on January 1, but you pay off your loan early, on June 30? On June 30, you will pay the $1,000 principal plus the accrued interest at that time, which would be $30. It really cost you $90 to borrow that money. As a practical matter, your true interest rate is 18%. It cost you $90 to borrow $1,000 for a half year. That is 18% interest.

When lenders quote APR to you, their calculations are based on the assumption that you will keep the loan and make payments for the entire term, even if that is thirty years. Most people do not keep their loans for thirty years—they either refinance the property or sell the property and pay off the loan. By analogy to the $1,000 example, you can see that if you plan to keep a loan in place for less than the full term, your true APR might actually be much higher.

This is important because one lender might quote you a low interest rate on a thirty-year loan, with high up-front fees, resulting in an APR of 9.5%. Remember, the rate of 9.5% is reached by assuming you will keep the loan in place for thirty years. Another lender might have a somewhat higher interest rate, a ten-year term, much lower up-front fees, and an APR of 9.75%. To compare apples to apples, you cannot simply compare the 9.5% to the 9.75%. You must ask each lender to calculate the APR using a hypothetical term that is equal, such as ten years or thirty years. While you are at it, ask the lender to calculate the APR if you pay off the loan early, such as five years from now. If he or she is uncooperative, you can go to websites such as **www.moneytoys.com** or **www.efunda.com** and calculate the numbers yourself.

What are prepayment penalties?

Some loans contain provisions requiring you to pay a penalty if you pay the loan off earlier than agreed or if you make larger principal reductions than the lender planned. If there is a penalty, it is generally only during the first few years of the loan. Sometimes it is a percentage of the loan balance at that time, and other times the penalty is six to twelve months of interest. The reasoning is that a lender counts on receiving an income stream for a certain period of time. If it receives its principal early, then it must loan it to someone else as quickly as possible. That might not happen immediately, and it will almost always require some marketing and administrative expenses.

Why might I want a fully amortizing loan?

The most common type of mortgage loans today are *fully amortizing loans*, which involve regular monthly payments that will eventually pay the loan in full over a specified amount of time. Thirty-year terms are the most widespread, although some longer terms are now allowed, such as forty- and fifty-year mortgages.

Many people think that shorter loan terms are better, as they will save the borrower several thousands of dollars in interest over the life of the loan. Over the course of thirty years, a $100,000 mortgage at 6% interest will result in $115,838 in interest, with payments of $599.55 per month. For the recommended twenty-year term, total interest drops to $71,943.20 but payments increase to $716.43 per month.

However, most Americans keep their homes less than ten years. This means that as a practical matter, the property is sold and the loan is paid off long before the completion of the term, so people can actually save money by not taking out a loan with a shorter term but higher monthly payments.

What is a balloon loan?

Balloon mortgages, also called *partially amortizing loans*, offer monthly payments calculated as if the loan would be fully amortizing, but the entire principal balance will be due in a shorter time, usually five, seven, or ten years. Commercial lenders will usually say, "I can offer you a ten-year loan on a thirty-year am," meaning a ten-year loan but with monthly payments calculated is if it were a thirty-year loan. Residential lenders usually call this a balloon mortgage. You can usually obtain somewhat cheaper rates with balloon loans than if you had a fully amortizing thirty-year loan.

Often, you have the option to convert the loan to a regular mortgage at the market rate for thirty-year loans, *plus* a little bit of extra interest, usually 3/8%. If you have a five-year balloon with a conversion option, the loan is called a 5/25 Convertible. For seven-year balloons, it is called a 7/23 Convertible.

What is the difference between an adjustable rate mortgage and a variable rate mortgage?

Home lenders generally offer adjustable rate mortgages. Business lenders (those who loan to flippers or rental income investors) usually offer variable rate mortgage loans.

An adjustable rate mortgage (ARM) changes interest rates only on certain anniversary dates, such as once every six months or once per year.

Variable rate loans change interest rates every time the index changes. If your variable rate loan is based on something called the 11th District Cost of Funds Index, then every single time that rate changes, your loan interest will also change. That means your payments could be different amounts every month. Many times, variable rate loans have a *floor*, which means your interest rate may not decrease below a certain percentage, even if the index rate drops dramatically.

How can I protect myself against high interest rates under an ARM?

You should make sure that your ARM has *interest rate caps*. This is a promise by the lender that interest rates will not increase more than a certain percentage each year, and will not increase more than a certain percentage over the lifetime of the loan. Not all ARMs have such caps. Almost no variable rate loans have caps.

Does an ARM payment cap protect me against high payments?

Some ARM loans have *payment caps*, meaning your monthly payment cannot increase above a certain amount, even if the interest rate rises sharply. The danger is something called *negative amortization*. Suppose your payment cap is $500 per month, but your interest rate increase should have resulted in a payment of $550 per month. Your lender does not just forgive the extra $50 in interest. No, your lender takes that $50 per month out of your equity! Rather than amortizing your loan so the principal balance gets lower each month, you are negatively amortizing and your principal balance is getting higher every month.

Can I get a VA loan for my foreclosure purchase?

The Veterans Administration (VA) will guarantee certain owner-occupied residential loans made by banks or other lenders. Investors and flippers need not apply.

The guarantee is limited to qualified veterans, up to a maximum guarantee amount of $50,750. The Veterans Administration does not actually loan the money directly. Most lenders require that the VA guarantee, along with a down payment from the buyer, equal at least 25% of the value—or purchase price, whichever is less—of the home. The eligibility rules for length of service are rather compli-cated and range from ninety days to six years, depending on the circumstances, timing, whether it is war time or peace time, and the borrower's status as active duty, member of the National Guard, etc. For more information, contact the Veterans Administration at **www.va.gov** or 1-800-827-1000.

With a VA guarantee, lenders can approve somewhat riskier loans at lower interest rates and with little or no down payment. In addi-tion, borrowers can qualify, even though up to 41% of their income is used for debt service. This is higher than typical underwriting requirements for non-VA loans.

The borrower must live in the home and not use it for rental income, be a satisfactory credit risk (under lenient VA guidelines), and have a stable source of income. In order to obtain the guarantee, the veteran will usually have to pay a 2% fee, and eligible Reserve/National Guard members will have to pay a 2.75% fee. These fees can be reduced by paying a down payment; any lender or broker can help you with the details.

You will need a *Certificate of Eligibility* to qualify for a VA guar-antee. If you do not already have one, it can be obtained from your local VA office by completing VA Form 26-1880, *Request for a Certificate of Eligibility*. You will also need a VA appraisal, called a *certificate of reasonable value* (CRV). The lender usually orders one. Otherwise, the process is pretty much the same as it is for any other loan, except that you must advise your lender that you want a VA guarantee.

Are FHA loans available for foreclosure purchases?

Yes, but only if you plan to occupy the property as your principal residence. The Federal Housing Administration (FHA) is a part of the Department of Housing and Urban Development (HUD). The FHA has a goal of increasing homeownership among low-income and middle-income Americans. To encourage it, the FHA insures certain loans made by lenders. The FHA does not make any loans itself. Because of the insurance, however, lenders are able to stretch a bit and loan money to people who might not otherwise qualify.

These loans are not limited to borrowers with credit problems or low income, but they do assist those who might otherwise not be able to obtain financing. Starting with loans made on or after January 1, 2008, the borrower-paid insurance premium will depend on your credit score. The lower your credit score, the more you will pay to obtain the FHA insurance.

If there are financial blemishes in your life, the following are the requirements in addition to paying the insurance premium.

- Qualified borrowers must have been discharged from bankruptcy at least two years earlier, been paying on a Chapter 13 plan for at least twelve months, or had a foreclosure no more recently than three years earlier.

- All judgments must have been paid in full before closing, but collections accounts do not have to be paid if you have *mitigating factors* (a good excuse).

- Usually, you must have a history of four or more creditors with regular payments on your credit report. If you do not have that many, you can use evidence of timely rent payments, utilities, or car insurance.

The required down payment on an FHA-insured loan is usually only 3%, and the money can be a gift from someone else. There is an exception for homeowners who lost their property in regions declared a federal disaster area by the president. Those borrowers can obtain 100% financing. Disaster victims do not have to buy property in the same area; they can relocate, if they want.

How can I calculate my monthly payments?

A wide variety of websites have online financial calculators that let you input your loan amount, interest rate, and loan term. The calculator will tell you what your monthly payments will be. I can recommend **www.bankrate.com**, and the AOL web page at **http://money.aol.com/mortgage**.

If you do not always have easy access to the Internet, you can do the same calculations in Microsoft Excel. Create a spreadsheet as follows. Column A has the information you will enter on your spreadsheet for each row. You must enter the information in exactly the order described; otherwise, you will not arrive at the right monthly payment.

	A	Explanation	Example
1	[Enter your info]	Amount of loan with no commas	119000
2	[Enter your info]	Term, in years	30
3	[Enter your info]	Annual interest rate, expressed as a decimal (7% is 0.07)	0.07
4	=pmt(A3/12,A2*12,-A1)	Enter this formula exactly as written. There are no spaces between anything.	Answer: $791.71

Chapter 8

WHAT YOU SHOULD KNOW ABOUT TAXES

- Will the IRS let me use my IRA retirement money to help buy a foreclosure property?
- Can I use money from my 401(k) to buy a home or an investment property for flipping or rental income?
- Can I deduct my mortgage payments from my taxes?
- How much money will I save with the interest deductions? Will the savings allow me to buy a more expensive property?
- How can owning investment real estate reduce my income taxes?
- What is depreciation?
- What are some other deductions?
- Is there a downside to depreciation deductions?
- Are there any limits on my deductions?
- What is the Alternative Minimum Tax?
- What are the passive activity rules?
- What are the most common tax credits?
- Can I take advantage of long-term capital gains tax rates?
- What is a 1031 (tax-free) exchange?
- I heard that short sales, which involve convincing a lender to take less than the full payoff for a mortgage loan, can cause tax problems. Is that true?

Will the IRS let me use my IRA retirement money to help buy a foreclosure property?

You must be a first-time home buyer, but the IRS has a very liberal definition of *first-time home buyer*.

Generally speaking, first-time home buyers can withdraw up to $10,000 from their Individual Retirement Arrangments (IRA) or Roth IRA accounts, penalty-free, in order to pay qualified home purchase expenses such as a down payment. Spouses can withdraw up to $20,000. There is a lifetime limit, though. Once you use up your distribution free passes, you cannot put the money back in your account and then use it again in the future. Remember, too, that you still have to pay taxes on the money, but not the 10% early withdrawal penalty.

According to the IRS, a *first-time home buyer* is someone who has not bought a home in the last two years, or the spouse, parent, child, or other relative of such a person. In other words, your grandmother can withdraw up to $10,000 from her IRA to help you buy a house as long as you have not bought a home in the last two years.

For more information, go to **www.irs.gov** or call 800-TAX-FORM and get a copy of Tax Topic 428 (Roth IRA Distributions) and Publication 590 "Individual Retirement Arrangements."

Can I use money from my 401(k) to buy a home or an investment property for flipping or rental income?

Although you cannot distribute money from your 401(k) program penalty-free or tax-free, you may be able to borrow money from it. Your ability to borrow will depend on whether your particular plan documents allow it. In order to qualify, such loans must meet *all* the following requirements.

- You must borrow less than 50% of your vested account, or $50,000, whichever is less.

- The loan must be repaid within five years, unless the money is used to buy your primary residence.

- Loan payments must be substantially equal, and payments must be made at least quarterly. You cannot pay $1 per year for five years, with all the accrued interest and principal due at the end of the loan repayment schedule.

There are some other technical requirements, such as reductions on the $50,000 limit if you already have outstanding loans from your 401(k). Ask your plan administrator for details.

Can I deduct my mortgage payments from my taxes?

You can deduct the interest portion of your mortgage payments whether the loan is for residential or business purposes. There are limits for home mortgage interest, however.

Currently, only the interest on $1,000,000 worth of home mortgage debt is deductible. Fortunately, most of us do not need to worry about this problem.

Home equity line of credit interest is deductible on only $100,000 worth of debt. You can have more debt than that, but you can only deduct the interest on the first $100,000 portion.

Second home interest is also deductible. However, your combined mortgage debt is limited to that $1,000,000 ceiling.

You can read more information on deducting mortgage payments in IRS Publication 936, "Home Mortgage Interest Deduction." For more information on the mechanics and details of homeownership deductions in general, refer to IRS Publication 530, "Tax Information For First-Time Homeowners." You can download these from the Web at **www.irs.gov/publications**, or you can call 800-TAX-FORM.

How much money will I save with the interest deductions? Will the savings allow me to buy a more expensive property?

Your tax savings will depend on how much interest you are going to pay and what tax bracket you are in. Tax brackets change each year. They are based on your filing status (married, single, etc.) and your adjusted gross income level. The brackets are prorated, so even if you are in a higher tax bracket, part of your income is still taxed at the lower percentage.

For homeowners, I generally do not recommend counting on income tax savings to help support a higher monthly mortgage payment than originally planned. This is because there are usually many unexpected expenses with homeownership, so your tax savings need to be reserved for those items.

Flippers usually do not hold property long enough to generate any tax advantages. Investors who buy for the long term may enjoy significant tax savings through interest deductions, ownership expenses, and depreciation deductions. The combination of all three may make seemingly expensive properties much more affordable.

The IRS has an excellent tax calculator at **www.irs.gov**. The information you enter into the calculator is completey confidential. You do not enter your name, and the IRS cannot tell who you are. All information is deleted as soon as you exit.

How can owning investment real estate reduce my income taxes?

There are five fundamental ways that owning investment real estate can reduce your income taxes.

1. Depreciation deductions each year allow you to write off part of the cost of your investment, which results in lower taxable income and lower taxes. If you have a $1,000 tax deduction, $1,000 of your income will be tax-free. This is called *sheltering*. Tax shelters are not just for the rich.

2. Virtually all expenses associated with owning and operating investment properties, including mortgage interest, are deductible.

3. Some real estate investments give you tax credits. *Tax credits* are used to reduce your tax liability. Dollar for dollar, these are more valuable than deductions. If you are in the 28% tax bracket, then a $1,000 tax credit means that $3,571.43 of your income will be tax-free (28% of $3,571.43 is $1,000). You would have to pay $1,000 in taxes on $3,571.43, but the tax credit wipes out your tax liability.

4. With capital gains tax rates, you can sell real estate after owning it for one year and pay taxes at a greatly reduced rate. Right now, the highest tax rate for an individual's ordinary income (wages, salary, rents from property, interest, dividends, etc.) is 35%. The highest capital gains tax rate is only 15%. Flippers usually cannot take advantage of capital gains tax rates. This is discussed more later.

5. Under certain circumstances, you can sell investment real estate, buy another property in a fairly short amount of time, and pay no income taxes on your profit! This is called a *1031* (ten–thirty-one) *exchange* and is discussed in more detail later.

What is depreciation?

Technically, *depreciation* is an accounting term. The IRS equivalent that gives you tax deductions is called *cost recovery*. You will need to know both terms if you are doing Internet research. In common speech, though, everyone just calls both of them *depreciation*.

Depreciation deductions are available to investors, not to homeowners.

Depreciation is an agreed-upon fiction that your real estate improvements (not the land itself, but everything else) are becoming less valuable every year at a steady rate. The IRS is of the opinion that residential rental properties will last for 27.5 years after you buy or build them and then be worthless. The IRS allows you to pretend that commercial properties will last for 39 years, and convenience stores will have no value after 15 years. As a result, you are allowed to write off, as a deduction, the pro rata amount that the property loses in value each year.

You can increase your deductions if you take advantage of something called *cost allocation depreciation*. With this, some components of your property improvements can be split out and depreciated more quickly than the whole. Carpets, exterior lighting, fencing, security systems, and other items can be depreciated over five, seven, or fifteen years, for example. Talk to an accountant or do a good bit of research before taking this route, however. Guessing can result in audits, fines, and penalties.

What are some other deductions?

Virtually everything associated with operating, insuring, protecting, repairing, or managing investment real estate can be deducted as an expense. Some items that add to the property or extend its life, such as a new roof or a building addition, cannot be deducted. Instead, you have to depreciate them a little bit each year. This is an area that might require some accounting assistance. For a general overview, read IRS Publication 527, "Residential Rental Property," and Publication 946, "How to Depreciate Property," for more details. They are available at **www.irs.gov** to download, or by calling 800-829-1040 to request a mailed copy.

Is there a downside to depreciation deductions?

There is not really a downside, but just a consequence that many people do not really think about. It makes logical sense, once someone explains it, but it might not occur to you ahead of time.

Suppose you pay $65,000 for a rental house. You own it for exactly one year, and then you sell it for $65,000. There is no gain, so you have no taxable income on the transaction.

But what if you owned it for a little over one year and wrote off $2,000 of depreciation deductions? You get the benefit of $2,000 worth of tax benefits in the current year. The IRS will not let you sell the property for $65,000 and pay no income taxes. It says, "You received $2,000 worth of tax benefits last year, so we are going to take back some of those benefits this year."

For purposes of calculating gain on the sale, you have to subtract that $2,000 from your $65,000 purchase price and treat the property as if you bought it for only $63,000. This is called your *basis*. Every year that you take depreciation deductions (but not any other normal expenses), you have to reduce your basis in the same amount as the depreciation deductions. In the example, you sell the property for $65,000 and you had a basis of $63,000, so your gain is $2,000.

You might think that the depreciation does not help you at all. It really does, though. You receive tax deductions against each year's taxable income. You save money at your highest tax rate for that year. Yes, you pay taxes in a later year when you sell the property, but that is in the future when inflation makes your dollars cheaper. Also, if you qualify for long-term capital gains tax rates, then the highest rate is 15% instead of the highest individual tax rate of 35%. As a result, your deductions save you money at 35%, and paying taxes later costs you only 15%, so you really do win. Furthermore, if you use a 1031 exchange, then you do not have to pay any taxes at all, even when you sell the property!

Are there any limits on my deductions?

There are two limits on your deductions. One is caused by calculations performed under the *Alternative Minimum Tax* rules, called Alt-Min for short. The other has to do with something called the *passive activity* rules. Neither one of these rules affects how much your property deductions can reduce your property income. They both affect how much *other* income you can shelter with your real estate deductions.

What is the Alternative Minimum Tax?

Under the *Alternative Minimum Tax* (Alt-Min), certain tax deductions, called *tax preference items*, are given limited effect. Depreciation is a tax preference item. The law was passed in 1969 in order to prevent a few wealthy individuals from escaping income taxes completely by virtue of their many deductions. It was pretty much a public relations ploy and was very popular with most Americans. The rules never changed to account for inflation, however. The annual income of a wealthy individual in 1969 is a normal two-earner income in today's world. This means that average Americans are being caught in the Alt-Min trap. The *New York Times* estimates that by 2010, nearly thirty million Americans will have to pay additional taxes because of Alt-Min.

The Alt-Min calculations are complex. Fortunately, the IRS provides an electronic worksheet, called the "Alternative Minimum Tax Assistant for Individuals," at **www.irs.gov**. It lets you manipulate your numbers to see what happens. Do not worry—your identity is protected on this website. No information will be collected and matched against your actual tax returns later. You can also download Tax Topic 556, "Alternative Minimum Tax," for a better under-standing of the rules.

What are the passive activity rules?

The IRS makes a distinction between certain types of income and expenses, especially those it considers a result of so-called *passive activities. Passive activity expenses* are deductible only from *passive activity income*. If expenses exceed income, then the losses cannot be used to offset other income, such as payroll income. Instead, the passive activity losses have to be carried forward and used in future tax years. Rental activities are considered passive activities. For example, if you have $35,000 of expenses associated with rental properties (because of depreciation deductions) and only $12,000 of income, then you will pay no taxes on the $12,000. However, you cannot use the leftover $23,000 to reduce the taxable income from your day job.

The good news is that there are three exceptions.

1. Taxpayers may deduct up to $12,500 in passive losses (up to $25,000 for married couples) if they or their spouses actively participated in the real property activity.

2. If the rental is a dwelling that the taxpayer uses for more than fourteen days per year or 10% of the days the dwelling is available for rental (whichever is greater), then it does not count as a passive activity. This would be your beach house, for example.

3. The taxpayer is a real estate professional, which, for these purposes, means someone who performed more than 750 hours of services that year in real property trades or businesses in which he or she materially participated, and more than half the personal services the taxpayer performed in all trades or businesses was performed in real property trades or businesses.

That is a lot of technical IRS language. Converting it into plain English would take more pages than I can devote to the subject here. For more information, see IRS Publication 925, "Passive Activity and the At-Risk Rules," and Tax Topic 425, "Passive Activities—Losses and Credits," at the IRS website, **www.irs.gov**.

What are the most common tax credits?

While I cannot get into the specific requirements here, you can do your own research once you know of the existence of these tax credits. Remember, a *tax credit* reduces your bottom line tax liability. One dollar in tax credits saves you one dollar in taxes. That is different from a *deduction* (like depreciation or operating expenses), in which a one-dollar deduction might save you fifteen cents to thirty-five cents in taxes.

The three most common tax credits available to investors in real estate are as follows.

1. Rehabilitation tax credits for fixer-uppers.

2. Energy efficiency tax credits for installing energy efficient systems and appliances.

3. Low-income housing tax credits are a time-consuming but extremely profitable strategy. Although the credits are for your federal income taxes, you must call your state low-income housing agency for more details. The IRS gives the credits to the states, and then the states award them to applicants. See also HUD information available at **www.huduser.org/datasets/lihtc.html**.

Can I take advantage of long-term capital gains tax rates?

Yes, any investor (but not homeowner or flipper) can take advantage of the reduced capital gains tax rates, as long as the rules are followed. If you own property for a certain minimum period of time before selling it, you can pay taxes at a reduced rate on the gain. Currently, the highest tax rate for long-term capital gains is 15%. For short-term capital gains (property held one year or less) or for other ordinary income, the highest rate is 35%.

To qualify for long-term capital gains rates, you must hold the property for more than one year. This does not mean exactly one year, but rather more than one year. The first day is considered the day after you acquired the property. The day you sell it is counted as part of the holding period. If you buy on January 1, 2008, then January 2, 2008, counts as the first day of the holding period. If you sell on January 1, 2009, then that is exactly one year that you have held the property, and you do not get capital gains treatment.

What is a 1031 (tax-free) exchange?

The *1031 exchange* (pronounced ten–thirty-one), also called a *Starker exchange* or a *like-kind exchange*, is a way of selling real estate and not paying any taxes until sometime in the (hopefully) distant future. Many people call it a tax-free exchange, but the more correct expression would be *tax-deferred exchange*.

Thanks to Mr. Starker, who was the first person to win on this issue against the IRS, you can avoid paying taxes at the time you sell property, but only if you follow the IRS rules exactly. There is no room for error. You will almost always need to hire a professional to handle these details for you, but the tax savings will more than pay for the professional fees.

First, you sell your property. The sold property is called the *relinquished property*. All the sale proceeds must be kept in escrow by someone called a *qualified intermediary*. Usually, this is a closing attorney or escrow company. You have 45 days from the sale of your relinquished property to identify the new real estate you want to buy, called the *replacement property*. You officially identify the property by giving a written statement to the qualified intermediary. You can pick up to three properties to identify, but you must buy one of those properties within 180 days of the sale of your relinquished property or by the due date of the tax return for the year of your sale, whichever occurs first.

If you do everything exactly right, you do not pay any taxes for the year on the sale of your relinquished property. The technical details regarding other requirements can get pretty complicated. For more information, you might want to read Publication 544, "Sales and Other Dispositions of Assets," and Form 8824, "Like-Kind Exchanges," both available at **www.irs.gov**.

I heard that short sales, which involve convincing a lender to take less than the full payoff for a mortgage loan, can cause tax problems. Is that true?

The tax problems are for the borrower, not for you. The IRS says that if someone owes money and the creditor forgives that debt, it is the same as earning income in the amount of the debt forgiven. Suppose a borrower owes $120,000 on her home. Facing foreclosure, she agrees to sell it to you for $100,000. The lender agrees to accept only $100,000 and to forgive the remaining $20,000. According to the IRS, the borrower will have a taxable income of $20,000.

The *Mortgage Relief Cancellation Act of 2007* proposes to change this rule, at least in the context of foreclosures and sales made to avoid foreclosure. While it was introduced in April 2007, as of the writing of this book, the law has not moved out of committee. Until it gets passed into law, you may want to remember the simple loophole. It may be necessary to explain the loophole in order to gain borrower's assistance for a short sale.

Simply said, the IRS states that there will be no taxable income if the borrower was *insolvent* before the debt forgiveness and he or she was still insolvent after the debt forgiveness—in other words, his or her debts were greater than his or her assets. The borrower may need to keep records regarding his or her insolvency in case there is an audit in the future. If you are interested in this subject, read IRS Publication 908, "Bankruptcy Tax Guide," available at your post office, local IRS office, or online at **www.irs.gov**. The advice in this form is not limited to bankruptcy situations.

Chapter 9

BANKRUPTCY AND FORECLOSURE

- What is bankruptcy?
- How can the bankruptcy laws affect my foreclosure buying?
- Can I follow the process of bankruptcy cases without hiring my own lawyer?
- What should I know about Chapter 7?
- What is important about Chapter 11 bankruptcies?
- What is Chapter 13?
- How does bankruptcy affect real estate?

What is bankruptcy?

Bankruptcy is an expression used to mean *insolvency*, which is a condition in which a person's liabilities exceed his or her assets, or in which current cash flow is not sufficient to meet current debts. As a result of the condition, the debtor may take advantage of protections afforded by the *Bankruptcy Code*.

Immediately upon filing for bankruptcy, the law imposes an automatic *stay* that prohibits all collection activities. Everything must stop at once, including foreclosures.

Over time, the stay may be lifted or suspended so that collection activities may resume. The law does allow a breathing spell to allow the debtor and his or her attorney time to analyze their options.

The Bankruptcy Code underwent a dramatic change with the *Bankruptcy Abuse Prevention and Consumer Protection Act of 2005* (BAPCPA.) Bankruptcy is now a much less consumer-friendly thing than it used to be, and it places greater demands on bankruptcy lawyers.

How can the bankruptcy laws affect my foreclosure buying?

Borrowers always have the option of seeking bankruptcy protection from their creditors. The decision can be made at the last possible moment, minutes before the fall of the auctioneer's gavel. Under some circumstances, completed foreclosures can even be reversed. You should have a good understanding of bankruptcy fundamentals so you know when to be worried, when to proceed full speed ahead, and when someone is bluffing you.

Can I follow the process of bankruptcy cases without hiring my own lawyer?

Bankruptcy case documents are now online and available to the public via the PACER System. The website is **http://pacer.psc.uscourts.gov**.

Access requires the use of a debit or credit card in order to set up an account. There is a charge of 8¢ per page for each document downloaded or viewed, with a maximum charge of $2.40 per document, no matter how large it is. You must know the name of the debtor to review his or her bankruptcy case. Usually, you will not need to see specific bankruptcy motions and orders, but only the docket sheet. The docket sheet is a listing of all documents filed in the case.

What should I know about Chapter 7?

A case brought under *Chapter 7* of the Bankruptcy Code has the goal of liquidating all assets, paying all liabilities as far as the money will go, and then obtaining a discharge for the debtor for the remaining liabilities so he or she can make a fresh financial start. Keep in mind that some debts cannot be discharged, such as judgments for money damages for fraud, payroll withholding taxes, intentional damage, domestic obligations, and other items. Also, because of past credit card abuses with debtors maxing out their credit cards and then filing for bankruptcy, there is now increased scrutiny of purchases prior to bankruptcy. Suspect purchases will be denied discharge.

Debtors requesting Chapter 7 relief must complete government-approved credit counseling before filing or within a short time afterward if it is an emergency. Debtors may be forced to enter Chapter 13 rather than Chapter 7 bankruptcy if a *means test* determines they have the ability to repay some debts over time.

Chapter 7 rarely stops a foreclosure; it merely slows things down. In the typical Chapter 7 case, the debtor will have little or no equity in the home. Rather than liquidate the property and turn the money over to the lender, the court will simply abandon the house and allow foreclosure to proceed. Do not be discouraged if a borrower enters Chapter 7. Be patient and keep track of the court proceedings.

What is important about Chapter 11 bankruptcies?

Chapter 11 is commonly called *reorganization*. It is designed for businesses or for individuals who exceed the financial limitations for Chapter 13 eligibility. Business owners may continue operations and propose a plan to meet their obligations, or they may form a plan to sell the business as a going concern rather than liquidate assets. The plans usually contemplate the sale of some assets, forgiveness of some debt, and a generous repayment schedule over time.

Things rarely work out well for the debtor, and the vast majority of Chapter 11 cases either result in the largest lender owning the company at the end, or the company changing its plan to one of liquidation. Just because the goal is liquidation does not mean the debtors must convert to Chapter 7; they are said to be in a *liquidating 11*.

You can buy property from the *Chapter 11 debtor-in-possession* (if the borrower remains in control of the case) or the *Chapter 11 trustee* (if the creditors take control). In both instances, any sale must receive court approval. A debtor with more than a few rental properties may be able to obtain a higher price selling the properties one at a time rather than offering the entire portfolio to another investor. This may present some true opportunities for potential homeowners and for foreclosure investors.

What is Chapter 13?

Chapter 13 is commonly called *wage earner bankruptcy*. The name is misleading because anyone with regular income from some source may take advantage of the chapter. There are financial limitations for eligibility that, if exceeded, will result in the debtor being forced to file Chapter 11 instead of Chapter 13.

The debtor proposes a plan for the repayment of debts, with payments stretching over three to five years. The plan can provide for the payment of past due mortgage payments over that time period, but current payments must be made currently. At the end of the time period, if all agreements under the plan have been met and if the debtor completes all required financial education, he or she receives a discharge.

How does bankruptcy affect real estate?

- Filing bankruptcy stops all foreclosure activities until and unless the lender is able to lift the automatic stay and obtain court approval to proceed. In some states where a debtor may redeem property after a foreclosure sale, the bankruptcy will enable the debtor to do so by making payments rather than by paying the full cash price ordinarily required for a redemption.

- Transfers of real estate within the recent past may be reversed if the transfers are for less than full value and deemed to be a fraud against creditors, even if there was no fraudulent intent. This includes preforeclosure sales like the ones you may be considering.

- Contracts to sell real property may be terminated or canceled depending on the type of bankruptcy filed.

- Commercial lenders, who typically require that collateral be held in a single asset entity, may be able to successfully argue against a plan of reorganization and force a foreclosure.

- Other lenders opposed to a Chapter 11 Plan of Reorganization may be forced to accept the plan in a procedure called the *cramdown.*

Chapter 10

THE FORMER OWNER

- How long should I give the former owner to remove his or her possessions?
- What do I do if the former owner will not vacate the property?
- Should I rent to the former owner?
- Is it a good idea to sell the property to the former owner and hold the financing?
- How do I sell my foreclosure property and hold the financing?
- What documents will I need if I agree to hold the financing for a house I sell?
- Can I rent out my house until I find a buyer?

How long should I give the former owner to remove his or her possessions?

State laws vary on this subject. Most will allow a former owner some period of time to remove his or her possessions without penalty. Some states that allow a post-foreclosure right of redemption—the right to buy the property back for the foreclosure bid price—say the right can be forfeited if the former owner does not vacate in a very short time. Be sure to check Appendix Three for resources that can tell you about the law in your area.

What do I do if the former owner will not vacate the property?

If the former owner does not vacate willingly, you will have to go through an eviction process similar to the one for tenants. Technically, it is called an unlawful detainer action, but you will find information under both names.

You cannot simply throw people's belongings out on the street, or you might find yourself on the receiving end of a lawsuit asking for damages against you. You might think you can carefully pack up the former owner's goods, deliver them to a self-storage place, pay the first month's rent, and let the former owner know where his or her stuff is located. While it might seem sensible, is also illegal in most states.

Instead, you will have to file a lawsuit and obtain a court order against the former owner. The order will give him or her a certain number of days to vacate the property. If the former owner does not do so, he or she will be in contempt of court. At that point, the judge usually orders local law enforcement to assist the former owner in leaving.

Again, the law is vastly different from state to state. It can also be extremely tricky. If you are up against someone knowledgeable, he or she might be able to hold you up for many months. Worse yet, the former owner might wait for you to make a mistake and then sue you for damages. Consult a good attorney if you find yourself having to get rid of a former owner. To educate yourself beforehand, you might want to check out some of these online resources.

- Apartments USA (**www.apartmentsusa.com**) has a website with loads of information about landlord/tenant issues (and eviction law) for each state.

- The Chiff.com directory (**www.chiff.com/legal/eviction laws.htm**), which pays for itself through advertising, has excellent resources about each state's eviction laws.

- The National Landlord Tenant Guides website (**www.rentlaw.com/eviction.htm**) is also very helpful.

Should I rent to the former owner?

Many foreclosure experts advise against this, and say you are only asking for trouble. Others swear by it, and say the former owner will make the best tenant, will take the best care of the property, and will probably stay the longest. You just have to evaluate your property, your former owner, and your tolerance for risk. Any tenant is a potential problem. If you are not comfortable with that thought, you should flip your foreclosure purchase rather than think about renting it out.

Is it a good idea to sell the property to the former owner and hold the financing?

You will find experts on both sides of this question. As a practical matter, the former owner will not have any down payment money at all. So, you will have to plan on holding the financing for 100% of the debt. One lender already got in trouble with that arrangement. Do you want to be the next one? If you do, you might want to use an arrangement called a land sale contract, contract for deed, or bond for title.

Those are all different names for the same arrangement. The seller keeps the deed to the property. The buyer makes some sort of down payment, and then makes monthly payments. The plan might call for payments for several years and then a refinance with a traditional lender. Or, the seller might hold the financing for the long term. The characteristic aspect of all these is that the buyer does not receive a deed until they have made all payments on time, and the purchase price paid in full.

This is a dangerous arrangement for buyers in many states because the financing terms say that if the buyer misses one payment or is late by even one day on a payment, the seller can declare a default. If there is a default, the contract ends immediately. There is no grace period. There is no foreclosure to go through, during which the buyer might do something to save the property. Chapter 13 Bankruptcy by the buyer cannot resurrect the arrangement and save their equity in the property.

Buyers with few choices will often enter into a contract for deed, though, because they have high hopes. Many sellers find the mechanism popular because they depend on the fact that the buyer will default. In the meantime, the seller obtains some sort of a down payment, plus higher monthly payments than they would be able to obtain as rent, plus the buyer usually fixes up the property and improves it. The buyer loses a substantial amount if there is a default, and the seller benefits.

For that reason, many states have consumer protections for buyers in such arrangements. After the buyer has made a certain number of payments, the law might reclassify the parties as traditional lender/borrower with a mortgage. This means that the buyer's equity will be protected in the same ways that any other borrower's equity is protected when they are faced with foreclosure. Other states, however, are very harsh on buyers in this situation. They uphold the right of the seller to declare a default, even when the buyer sacrifices substantial equity as a result. For your state laws, contact some of the resources listed in Appendix Three.

How do I sell my foreclosure property and hold the financing?

There are two methods of selling a home and holding the financing. Both require the cooperation and approval of your lender. You probably borrowed money on a short-term basis to acquire the house and then flip it fairly quickly. Things are now different. You and your lender will need to agree on a longer term for your loan, with regular monthly payments. Because almost all mortgages contain a due on sale clause, which makes the loan due in full if the property is sold, you will need an agreement by your lender to waive that clause.

The first financing method is a traditional sale, in which you give the buyer a deed and he or she takes the property subject to your lender's first mortgage. The buyer also gives you a mortgage, which wraps around the first mortgage. The buyer makes payments to you, and you then make payments to your lender.

Beware, however, that there are severe tax consequences if you do not structure this exactly right. In a nutshell, if the buyer makes payments directly to your lender, or does anything to make sure his or her payments to you will result in payments to your lender, you could owe huge taxes without having the cash to pay them. That is because the IRS will take the position that you made all your profit in the year of the sale, even though your money will come in spread over several years. With normal seller financing, the seller splits each mortgage payment into two parts—a refund of his investment and a profit on his investment. Only the profit portion of each payment is taxable during that year. A seller who spends $120,000 to buy and fix up a house, and then sells it for $180,000 and holds the financing, might have only a few hundred dollars of taxable profit in the first year. A seller who does a wrap-around mortgage, and who does not follow the IRS rules exactly, will have $60,000 of taxable profit in the first year. Please consult a tax professional for advice on how to avoid this consequence with proper planning.

The second popular method of seller financing for flippers is the contract for deed, also called a bond for title and sometimes a land sale contract. In this arrangement, the buyer does not receive a deed to the property until he or she has made all payments in full. It is a good arrangement for the seller because if the buyer defaults the seller can usually evict the buyer immediately. There is no lengthy foreclosure process, and even a last-minute bankruptcy will generally not save the purchaser and allow him or her to remain in the property. Those are the same factors that make this very risky for buyers. As a result, usually only the most desperate buyers, or the most unsophisticated ones, will agree to such an arrangement. The process is strongly disfavored by many states and courts because of the high risk that a buyer might forfeit substantial equity as a result of a minor default. For that reason, some states have consumer protection laws that heavily regulate such relationships and provide safety nets for defaulting buyers. Be sure to check Appendix Three at the back of this book, call your state's real estate department or consumer affairs office, and find out the law in your jurisdiction.

What documents will I need if I agree to hold the financing for a house I sell?

Please consult with a local attorney to answer this question. All states are different. At the very least, traditional financing will require a promissory note and a mortgage or a deed of trust, depending on your state. You might want to include a security agreement and a UCC-1, to cover anything on the property that might possibly be classified as personal property instead of real property, such as a swing set or portable storage building.

Obtain a copy of the documents for your own home. Do not use the mortgage on your flip property because that is classified as a commercial loan. The bank uses different forms, and has different legal requirements, for commercial loans than for home loans. The reason you want to look at some bank forms is because they are usually very strongly written in favor of the lender. Forms you obtain from a book, or off the Internet, or even from an attorney, might be less protective of your interests. Read everything, and compare the bank's documents to the ones you propose to use. Are there any clauses you should add? Is there anything you do not understand? Make sure you understand what you are signing, and are comfortable with it.

You will also need something in writing from your lender waiving the due on sale clause. You must have this in writing. It is not a matter of trusting your loan officer or not. If he or she transfers, has a promotion, changes employers, or retires, someone else will be in charge of your loan. In many circumstances, the bank is not bound by anything that is not in writing and part of their books and records. In other words, if you and your original loan officer both swear under oath that you can sell the house without paying off the loan, the bank can still say, "We don't care, it doesn't bind us." They can call your note, demand payment in full, and proceed to foreclosure if you do not pay up.

To be on the safe side, I would also obtain something in writing from an accountant or other tax professional that your documents meet IRS requirements so you do not have large taxable income in the year of the sale. A piece of paper, asking for a signature, tends to cause people to pay more attention and give more careful answers.

If you want to go the route of a contract for deed, go to the place were deeds are recorded in your jurisdiction. Often, people record contracts for deed in the real estate records. Obtain copies of several. Read them and make sure you understand the various clauses. Then hire an attorney to draft something for you, and compare the final product to the forms you copied. See if you need any changes in the finished product. As a practical consideration, I usually do not like to give people copies of forms I find. I think it structures their thinking, and prevents them from being creative and coming up with independent solutions. After the fact, I use my forms as a checklist, to make sure we've covered all the bases.

Can I rent out my house until I find a buyer?

Most flippers who are unable to sell quickly will put tenants in their properties. It has the benefit of providing monthly income to help pay your own holding costs—interest, taxes, and insurance. The tenant pays the utility bills. It keeps down your insurance costs because insurance for vacant houses is often much higher than for occupied homes. In addition, some theft and vandalism losses are often not covered at all if the property is vacant for some period of time.

Your lender will be much more willing to renew your note if you have a tenant in place. It shows that you have taken steps to minimize your losses, and acted in a business-like manner.

On the negative side, tenants can damage your property, making it harder to sell without spending more money for repairs. At the very least, the most careful tenant in the world will cause some wear and tear, meaning the house will no longer be move-in perfect for a new owner. On the other hand, very few buyers expect perfect homes, so that should not affect your sale price.

Another word of caution about tenants. An acquaintance of mine once rented a large home in a very desirable part of town. He lived there for several years, and then the owner decided to sell. My friend was paying rent substantially lower than similar properties in the market. Plus, he was nested in to the house and comfortable. He did not to move, but he also could not afford to pay the asking price. He did graciously offer to show the house to prospective buyers, so the owner would not have to drop everything each time someone called. On the morning of each showing, my acquaintance did three things. In the summer, he turned off the air conditioning and in the winter he turned off the heat. Next, he brought an overflowing cat litter box into the house, rather than its normal spot in a shed. Finally, he flipped a few circuit breakers so that, as he entered rooms and tried to turn on the lights, he could complain about the wiring and then correct the situation by flipping the circuit breaker back into the on position. The poor owner received no offers. After a year, she sold the house to the tenant at a deep discount. Don't let this happen to you!

That story also points out the biggest problem with tenants—they move into the house because they want to live in the house.

No one wants to sign a lease with a clause saying the landlord can kick him or her out if the house is sold. Normal landlords can pass that off as boilerplate, and say it is "just in case" but "not likely to happen." You will be different, because you will be actively trying to sell the property, from Day One. As a result, you might have problems attracting tenants.

One solution is to find a tenant, put them in place with a standard one-year lease, and then sell your house as a piece of income-producing property to an investor. That might or might not be a good strategy. Depending on where the house is located, an investor might pay more or less money than a homeowner. Be sure to research this issue before choosing this route. Also, most investors base their buying decisions on something called the Net Operating Income (NOI) from a property. In other words, what is the cash flow after receiving all the rent each year and then paying all expenses except mortgage payments. Obviously, the higher the rent, the larger the NOI and the more an investor will be willing to pay. You cannot put a tenant in the house at a discounted rent and then expect to sell the property based on what the rent should be with a different landlord.

Conclusion

Now that you know enough to start buying, get to it. You do not have to wait for the perfect property with the big paycheck at the end. Find something small that you can rent out easily and buy it. You will get your feet wet without suffering very much risk at all. At the same time, buying foreclosure properties will get into your blood. You will be ready for your next one before you have even closed on your first home.

Good luck!

Glossary

A

ad valorem tax. Literally means *according to the value*. It is a tax placed upon property and calculated with reference to the value of the property.

adverse possession. Under some circumstances, someone who uses your land for ten or twenty years—depending on the state and some technical details—and acts as if it is his or her own property, and can take it away from you legally.

after-tax equity yield. Methods of financial analysis for an equity position in real estate, being the net return rate on an investment after deducting expenses, interest, and taxes. For example, an investor buys a property with $100,000 down (equity) and $400,000 in financing. The investor receives $7,000 in cash flow each year, after paying income taxes on money earned from the investment. After five years, the investor sells the property and receives $150,000 after deducting taxes and sale costs. The investor receives a return of the original $100,000 and a sale profit of $50,000 upon sale, plus the $35,000 received over the course of five years, for a total of $185,000. After quantifying the various components, as described, you then calculate yield by using any of several formulas, such as cash-on-cash, internal rate of return, or any other method selected.

agent. Someone who represents someone else and can, under some circumstances, bind the person he or she represents to contracts. Real estate agents typically represent the sellers, even if they are "working with" them. Always ask who the agent represents. He or she may not have your best interests at heart!

appreciation. When real estate grows in value over the years.

C

certificate of occupancy. Certificate from a government department, usally the inspections department, approving a building for use. If you do not obtain a certificate of occupancy when one is required, you can be prohibited from using your property or renting it out to anyone else.

comparables method. A method of estimating value by comparing the subject property to similar properties that have sold in the recent past.

D

deed of trust. A security instrument by which real estate secures a promissory note.

deferred maintenace. Repairs that have been put off for awhile and are starting to pile up.

deficiency. The money a borrower might still owe his or her lender after a foreclosure if the property does not sell for enough money to pay the entire amount owed by the borrower to the lender.

depreciation. An accounting concept in which the IRS pretends that assets will decrease steadily in value over a predetermined time period until, at the very end of the period, they are completely worthless. It usually bears no relationship to reality, but it does allow you to write off expenses on your taxes even though you are not actually writing checks for those expenses.

due diligence. The research you should do to satisfy yourself that your potential purchase is as safe as possible.

duress. An extraneous pressure that causes people to sell property cheaply (because they are facing foreclosure) or causes other people to pay an unusually high price for property (in order to avoid income taxes).

E

eminent domain. The ability of the government to take property, whether the homeowner wants to sell or not.

equity. The difference between what a property is worth and what is owed on it. Just because someone pays $10,000 down to buy a property does not mean he or she still has $10,000 in equity. If the property appreciated, then the equity will be larger. If the property declined in value, then the equity will be smaller.

equity stripping. A term applied to a variety of sleight-of-hand practices, most often:

- offering to assist homeowners facing *foreclosure* through buying their home and then selling it back to them, usually at rates and on terms guaranteed to result in default and loss of all equity; and,

- protecting assets from creditors by encumbering the equity with loans from friendly creditors, such as relatives, who will not fore-close if the homeowner misses a few payments.

F

fair market value. The price that a willing buyer would pay a willing seller, with neither of them operating under duress.

G

guarantee. The act itself, or the document, whereby one agrees to pay a debt if the principal obligor does not. Formerly under common law, creditors had to exhaust their remedies against a debtor before pursuing a guarantor. Today, almost all guarantee instruments contain clauses allowing the creditor to seek payment directly from the guarantor if there has been a default by the debtor. Guarantee agreements must be in writing to be enforce-able. There must be some consideration passing to the guarantor unless the instrument creating the *obligation* (i.e., a lease) is signed at the same time as the guarantee, in which case the law assumes the guarantor has some interest in the transaction.

J

joint tenants. A method of property ownership. If a joint tenant sells his or her share to someone else, it destroys the joint tenancy and turns it into a tenancy in common. If a joint tenant dies, his or her share is split equally among the surviving joint tenants.

judicial foreclosure. Obtaining a court action in order to foreclose on real estate. This is required in some states.

L

lien. A generic name for claims against real estate. Lienholders can hold mortages, they can be creditors who filed judgments, or they might be taxing authorities like the IRS or a local government.

lis pendens. A notice placed in the real estate records that someone has a claim against property, even though the claim does not rise to the status of a lien. Heirs fighting over property might file lis pendens notices against each other. Spouses in the process of a divorce not yet finalized might file a lis pendens in order to give notice to potential purchasers or lienholders that someone else might own the property before too long, and that all buyers should beware.

M

mechanics' and materialmen's lien (M&M liens). A lien that suppliers and workers can place on property for the value of their goods and services if unpaid.

mortage. A security instrument by which real estate secures a promissory note.

N

nonjudicial foreclosure. Being able to foreclose on real estate without a court's assistance. This is only allowed in some states.

P

priority. A method of ranking lienholders to determine who gets the first money off the top of the sale, who gets the second amount, and so on. Except for very specialized circumstances in a bankruptcy, lienholders do not share money pro rata. Each one must be paid in full before the next one gets paid.

profit. Income you pay taxes on. Because the principal portion of mortgage payments does not qualify as an accounting or an IRS expense, you can have a paper profit but still not have enough money to pay your bills.

T

tenancy by the entireties. A method of property ownership for husbands and wives. One spouse is not allowed to sell his or her share unless both of them agree. No one, not even a divorce court, can take the property away from just one owner. If one spouse dies, the other one inherits that share.

tenants in common. A method of property ownership. Tenants in common share property, but no one has a particular piece. A tenant in common can sell his or her share to someone else. If a tenant in common dies, his or her heirs inherit his or her share.

title binder. A title binder says that if you do all the things the title company requires—like paying the purchase money and recording a deed—then the title company will issue title insurance when you pay the premium. A title binder is worthless if you do not complete all the steps and pay the premium.

title insurance. An insurance policy that pays off if it turns out that you do not have good and clear title to your property. Title insurance typically does not cover boundary line disputes or adverse possession claims. Lenders always require title insurance, but many buyers do not think to ask for coverage for themselves as well.

Torrens system. A method of registering the owner of real estate and all liens against the property. Torrens systems are voluntary.

triple net lease (NNN lease). A landlord/tenant arrangement in which the tenant pays all the expenses of property ownership, such as taxes, insurance, and maintenance. This is very common with commercial leases, and extremely uncommon with residential leases.

U

unlawful detainer. An eviction lawsuit.

W

write-down. A lender agreeing to take less than the full debt as payment in full.

SAMPLE BUSINESS PLAN

Your personal business plan should be updated at least once a year. You will have the most details for your one-year business plan. Those details will form your to-do list of what needs to be done in order to reach your one-year goals. You will have less detail about what is necessary to reach your two-, five- and ten-year goals, because those details will probably change dramatically over time. You should identify the additional goals, though, and think about what you will have to start doing today in order to reach those goals in the future.

Goals

By the end of one year from today

Purchase a foreclosure house to use as my personal residence. The house must have brick or vinyl siding, other low-maintenance features, three bedrooms and two bathrooms, and be in a good school district or near a college campus. The house must be suitable for conversion to rental property within three years, with monthly rental income (after expenses) at least equal to 120% of the mortgage payments.

By the end of two years from today

Own three rental houses in addition to my personal residence. [Or, own two rental houses in addition to your personal residence and complete two foreclosure flips with a profit of at least

$_____[X]_____ each, but make the profit number relatively small. You want low-risk flips while you are getting your feet wet, which usually means you will be making a relatively low profit.]

By the end of five years from today
Own five rental houses, quit my regular job, and work full-time on my real estate investments. Regularly do enough low-profit, quick-flips to at least equal my former annual salary and pay for health insurance and all other former benefits. [Or, have a sufficient number of rental properties to equal that number.] My gross annual income at the end of Year Five will be $_____[X]_____.

By the end of ten years from today
Sell all rental houses and buy an apartment complex. The apartment complex must provide enough revenue to pay the mortgage payments, all expenses including a 10% fee for a professional property management company, build up cash reserves for major repairs, and still generate annual cash flows of $_____[X]_____ so I can retire and do whatever I want, whenever I want.

Resources needed for one-year goals
Education
Read five foreclosure books and two flipping books by at least three different authors (in order to get different points of view and experiences). Decide on a specialty—preforeclosure, foreclosure auctions, postforeclosure—and learn everything necessary for that specialty. [Example: preforeclosure and foreclosure auctions as specialties will require that you learn how to research real estate titles yourself. You will need to quickly weed out anything that has no chance of working because of the number and size of other liens.] Take one community college night course relevant to my

plans, such as construction estimating, accounting, computer skills, etc.

Access to credit
Have a relationship with at least two lenders so I can quickly borrow $_____[X]_____ on a six-month, interest-only, promissory note.

Cash
Establish an investment savings account, and have at least $___[X]___, 70% of which will be available for any down-payments, and 30% of which will remain in the account for emergencies and surprise expenses.

Partners (family members or others)
I will have no outside partners, but my spouse will spend five hours a week assisting in reaching our goals. During those five hours a week, my spouse will: [examples: review home sale magazines and keep me updated regarding market rates, do online research regarding specific properties, or input data into my computer so I can build a database of property information and leads.]

Time (hours per week I can and will devote to this)
I will spend at least fifteen hours a week on this project. I will bring my lunch to work and read or search the Internet during my lunch break. I will get up a half hour earlier or go to bed a half hour later every day and spend that time reading, planning, or doing research. The remainder of my time commitment will be spent: _____. The significant people in my life have agreed with me that this is a reasonable time commitment and will support me in this regard.

Space

I will need the hall coat closet converted to a minioffice for myself, with a small file cabinet, a bookshelf, and a bulletin board. I can work on the kitchen table when I need to, but I will put all my stuff in my minioffice when finished.

Steps necessary to reach one-year goals

1. Set up my home office by _____[date]_____.

2. Read all books by_____[date]_____,

3. Complete all other described education by _____[date]_____.

4. Identify a partner who will supply things I do not have (additional time, cash, access to credit, and/or experience) and reach a formal agreement with that person regarding our relationship, even if that person is my spouse, child, or other relative.

5. Save $___[X]___ a month, or sell personal property I am willing to give up, in order to help reach my investing goals.

6. By _____[date]_____, know two lenders who have pre-approved me to borrow $_____[X]_____ within twenty-four hours of any request I make.

7. Choose three potential purchases by _____[date]_____. Imagine I will purchase all three of them, and gather all information I think will be necessary. Establish a budget, a purchase price, and a postpurchase plan. Follow the progress of the

properties to see what happens with them, and if things turned out the way I anticipated.

8. Find a potential purchase by _____[date]_____.

9. Find one potential purchase a month for each month after the date in step 8. This is in case the first purchase does not work out, so I will still have other opportunities in the pipeline.

10. Complete my first foreclosure purchase by _____[date]_____.

Steps necessary to reach two-year goals

[What additional cash, credit, education, time, partners, and space will you need to reach your two-year goals? Are there any baby steps you need to take in the first year in order to have those things by the end of the second year?]

Steps necessary to reach five-year goals

[What additional cash, credit, education, time, partners, and space will you need to reach your five-year goals? Are there any baby steps you need to take in the first year in order to have those things by the end of your fifth year?]

Steps necessary to reach ten-year goals

[What additional cash, credit, education, time, partners, and space will you need to reach your ten-year goals? Are there any baby steps you need to take in your first in order to have those things by the end of your tenth year?]

Appendix B

HUD GOOD NEIGHBOR NEXT DOOR

Reprinted from:
www.hud.gov/offices/hsg/sfh/reo/goodn/gnndabot.cfm

Law enforcement officers, pre-Kindergarten through 12th grade teachers, firefighters, and emergency medical technicians can contribute to community revitalization while becoming home-owners through HUD's *Good Neighbor Next Door Sales Program*. HUD offers a substantial incentive in the form of a discount of 50% from the list price of the home. In return you must commit to live in the property for thirty-six months as your sole residence.

How the Program Works
Eligible single-family homes located in revitalization areas are listed exclusively for sale through the Good Neighbor Next Door Sales program. Properties are available for purchase through the program for five days.

How to Participate in Good Neighbor Next Door
Check the listings for your state. Follow the instructions to submit your interest in purchasing a specific home. If more than one person submits on a single home a selection will be made by random lottery. You must meet the requirements for a law enforcement officer,

teacher, firefighter, or emergency medical technician, and comply with HUD's regulations for the program.

HUD requires that you sign a second mortgage and note for the discount amount. No interest or payments are required on this "silent second," provided that you fulfill the three-year occupancy requirement.

The number of properties available is limited and the list of available properties changes weekly.

Who Can Participate?

Law Enforcement

You may participate in the Good Neighbor Next Door program as a law enforcement officer if you are employed full-time by a law enforcement agency of the federal government, a state, a unit of general local government, or an Indian tribal government; and, in carrying out such full-time employment, you are sworn to uphold, and make arrests for violations of, federal, state, tribal, county, township, or municipal laws.

Teachers

You may participate in the Good Neighbor Next Door program as a teacher if you are employed as a full-time teacher by a state-accredited public school or private school that provides direct services to students in grades pre-kindergarten through 12. In addition, the public or private school where you are employed as a teacher must serve students from the area where the home you are purchasing is located in the normal course of business.

Firefighters and Emergency Medical Technicians

You may participate in the Good Neighbor Next Door program as a firefighter/emergency medical technician if you are employed full-time as a firefighter or emergency medical technician by a fire department or an emergency medical services responder unit of the federal government, a state, a unit of general local government, or an Indian tribal government serving the area where the home is located.

Revitalization Areas

Revitalization areas are HUD-designated neighborhoods in need of economic and community development and where there is already a strong commitment by the local governments. Revitalization areas are the basis for HUD programs such as the Good Neighbor Next Door Program and the Direct Sales Program for Nonprofit agencies and Municipalities.

There are hundreds of revitalization areas across the country. You may search for revitalization areas online. Property listings may be searched online at: **www.hud.gov/homes/index.cfm**.

Three-year Occupancy Requirement
Annual Certifications
When participants purchase properties under the Good Neighbor Next Door (GNND) program they agree with the program regulations to own and live in as their sole residence the property for a three-year period. Participants are required to certify every year that they are living in the property.

The annual certification is mailed to participants, ready for signature, around the anniversary of the purchase. Participants should sign, date, and return the form to the address specified in the letter. If they fail to return the first letter, a follow-up letter is sent one month later. At times, their return letter and our follow-up letter cross in the mail. If this happens, participants can either contact our servicer to determine if the first certification was received and logged in or they can sign and return the second certification.

If participants fail to return at least one annual certification per year, the National Servicing Center (NSC) refers the case for investigation. An investigator will then make an on-site visit to verify the occupancy of the property. Furthermore, the investigator will ask the participant to sign the annual certification in their presence. In the event that investigation fails to verify occupancy, the participant will be turned over to the Office of Inspector General for further investigation and possible prosecution. To avoid noncompliance, complete and return the annual certification forms promptly and honestly. Falsifying information on this certification is a felony. HUD will prosecute false claims and statements. Conviction may result in criminal and/or civil penalties. (18 USC 1001, 1010, 1012 3559, 3571; 31 USC 3729, 3802).

Military Duty

Participants that are called to active military duty are provided clemency in regard to the owner-occupancy requirements of the program for the time frame that they are in active duty. Participants on active military duty are not required to occupy the property and are allowed to rent the property (only while on active duty) if necessary to minimize potential vandalism. However, the NSC needs to be aware of those participants that are on active military duty and are not occupying their property. Participants must notify the NSC according to the Military Duty Instructions. Print out the information and instructions and comply with the instructions so that you will not be referred for investigation during your military duty.

Subordinations

When participants close on their home, they sign a note and a mortgage. The mortgage is filed right after the first (primary) mortgage, thereby making it a second mortgage. When participants pay off their first mortgage (usually done by refinancing), HUD's mortgage moves into first position. If a participant is attempting to refinance their first mortgage, the lender will want its new loan to be in first position. In order to accomplish this, HUD must be willing to subordinate its position to the new first mortgage.

HUD has certain rules and procedures regarding subordinating. The rules are that HUD will consent to refinancing (1) for the purpose of obtaining an FHA 203(k) rehabilitation loan or (2) for the purpose of obtaining a lower mortgage interest rate or change in the term of the loan and (3) to prevent the participant from defaulting on the first mortgage. The 203(k) loan is a rehabilitation loan in which necessary property improvements are financed into a new loan.

The closing (or title) agent handling the closing of the new loan should handle the paperwork and details to obtain the HUD subordination. Participants can refer the closing company to this page or they can print the "Subordination Information" sheet and take it to the closing company. Read the linked information then mail or fax the subordination request to our servicing subcontractor, Morris-Griffin/First Madison Services, Inc.

Payoffs

If a participant needs to dispose of the property before expiration of the three-year occupancy period (for job relocation, family composition changes, or refinance), NSC's subcontractor, Morris-Griffin/First Madison Services, Inc., processes those payoffs. Fax the request for the payoff with the following information: participant's name, full property address, estimated closing date, company requesting the payoff, company address, company telephone number, return fax number, and signed permission of the participant to collect the data. All of this information may be mailed or faxed to Morris-Griffin/First Madison Services, Inc. Payoff requests are usually processed and faxed out within two business days of receipt.

Releases

At the end of the required three-year occupancy period, HUD's second mortgage will be released provided:

1. the participant has completed and returned the required annual certifications;

2. is not currently under investigation by the Office of Inspector General; and,

3. is in compliance with all of the GNND regulations. A mortgage satisfaction will be filed with the participant's local county recorder's office. After the release is filed, a copy will be mailed to the property address. Thereafter, HUD's second mortgage will not show up on the title to your property. After release, there is no further obligation to or restrictions imposed by the Department of Housing and Urban Development. Releases are mailed to the county recorder for filing no later than thirty days after the end of the required occupancy period. However, some counties have a filing backlog and, therefore, HUD has no control.

Releases are prepared and filed by our servicing subcontractor, Morris-Griffin/First Madison Services, Inc.

STATE-SPECIFIC INFORMATION

Alabama

Foreclosure laws

Judicial vs. nonjudicial: Nonjudicial foreclosure predominates, but judicial foreclosure is allowed.

Notice period: 21 days

Right of redemption: One year after the auction

Deficiency judgments: Allowed

Law

Title 35 (Property) Articles 1, 1A, 2, 3 §35-10-1 et. seq.
http://alisdb.legislature.state.al.us/acas/ACASLogin.asp

Resources

Consumer Protection: www.ago.state.al.us/consumer.cfm

Disclosures: Alabama does not have state-specific disclosure laws and is, instead, a *caveat emptor* (buyer beware) state regarding sales of used property.

Local HUD Information: www.hud.gov/local/index.cfm?state=al

Alabama Real Estate Commission: www.arec.alabama.gov

Alabama Center for Real Estate: http://arerec.cba.ua.edu

University of South Alabama Real Estate Center:
www.southalabama.edu/publicrelations/pressreleases/2005pr/091205.html

Alaska
Foreclosure laws
Judicial vs. nonjudicial: Nonjudicial foreclosure typical.

Notice period: Sixty-five days. Must file notice of default in county where real estate is located, not less than thirty days after default.

Right of redemption: No redemption rights after foreclosure.

Deficiency judgment: None unless creditor sues on the note only.

Property owner can halt the process by bringing the loan current before the auction, unless he or she has done so twice before. In that case, the trustee can refuse the payment and proceed with the auction.

Law
Title 34 Alaska Statutes (Property) and Chapter 20 (Mortgages and Trust Deeds), Section 70 (Sale by Trustee), Section 80 (Sale at Public Auction)

http://touchngo.com/lglcntr/akstats/Statutes/Title34/Chapter20/Section070.htm

Resources
Consumer Protection: www.law.state.ak.us/department/civil/consumer/cpindex.html

Disclosures: www.dced.state.ak.us/occ/pub/rec4229.pdf

Local HUD Information: www.hud.gov/local/index.cfm?state=ak

Real Estate Commission: www.dced.state.ak.us/occ/prec.htm

Arizona

Foreclosure laws

Judicial vs. nonjudicial: Nonjudicial foreclosures are typical, but judicial foreclosures are allowed.

Notice period: Must be published once a week for four consecutive weeks before the date of the sale, and there must be at least ten days between the last publication and the sale date. Notice of the sale must be posted at the property within twenty days of the sale date. Notice of the sale must be recorded with the recorder of deeds at least ninety days before the sale.

Typical time period for a foreclosure: 120 days

Right of redemption: No postforeclosure right of redemption

Deficiency judgments: Allowed except where the security is a principal residence, or it is on 2.5 acres of land or less. Judgment is limited to the difference between the sale price and the fair market value of the property.

Law

Article 33, Chapters 6, 6.1 of Arizona Revised Statutes
www.azleg.state.az.us/ArizonaRevisedStatutes.asp?Title=33

Resources

Department of Real Estate: **www.re.state.az.us**
Disclosures: **www.re.state.az.us/PUBLIC_INFO/Documents/
Residential_Seller_Property_Disclosure_Statement.pdf
www.aaronline.com/documents/spds_samp.pdf**
Helpful links: **www.keytlaw.com/az/realestate/relawlinks.htm**
Local HUD Information: **www.hud.gov/local/index.cfm?state=az**
Arizona State University: **www.poly.asu.edu/realty**

Arkansas

Foreclosure laws

Judicial vs. nonjudicial: Both used equally, though moving more toward nonjudicial.

Notice period: Lender must file a *Notice of Default and Intention to Sell* in the country where the property is located. At least sixty days must elapse between the filing and any further foreclosure action. Foreclosure notice must be published for four weeks in a newspaper, with the last notice within ten days of the sale.

Typical time period for a foreclosure: 120 days

Right of redemption: None after a nonjudicial foreclosure. One year after a judicial foreclosure, but this can be waived in the loan documents.

Deficiency judgments: Allowed

Law

Arkansas Code, Title 18 (Property), Subtitle 4 (Mortgages And Liens) Chapter 49 (Enforcement of Mortgages, which deals with Judicial foreclosures) or Chapter 50, which deals with Statutory (nonjudicial) Foreclosures

http://170.94.58.9/NXT/gateway.dll?f=templates&fn=default.htm&vid=blr:code

Resources

Local HUD Information: www.hud.gov/local/index.cfm?state=ar

Real Estate Commission: www.state.ar.us/arec/arecweb.html

California
Foreclosure laws

Judicial vs. nonjudicial: Both, but nonjudicial foreclosures are more common.

Notice period: A *Notice of Default* is filed in the real estate records. Nothing else can occur for sixty days during the redemption period. After this, the lender records additional information in the real estate records, but it must be at least fourteen days before the sale (publication period).

Right of redemption: One year, unless lender made a full-price bid, in which case the time period is shortened to ninety days. There is no right of redemption if the lender waives a deficiency or if it is not allowed to obtain a deficiency under the circumstances.

Deficiency judgments: Not allowed with nonjudicial foreclosures, but allowed with judicial foreclosures. No deficiency is allowed under purchase money mortgages.

Law

California Civil Code, Section 2924
www.leginfo.ca.gov

Resources

Department of Real Estate: **www.dre.cahwnet.gov**

Local HUD Information: **www.hud.gov/local/index.cfm?state=ca**

California Department of Real Estate, Required Disclosures in Real Property Transactions: **www.dre.ca.gov/pub_disclosures.html**

California Department of Real Estate (with guides and information for consumers): **www.dre.ca.gov**

University of California (Berkeley): **http://groups.haas.berkeley. edu/realestate/**

University of Southern California: **www.usc.edu/schools/sppd/lusk/**

Colorado

Foreclosure laws

Judicial vs. nonjudicial: Nonjudicial

Notice period: Lender must file a *Notice of Election and Demand* with the state's public trustee. The trustee must file that notice in the real estate records within ten business days of receipt. A copy of the notice must be published in the newspaper for five consecutive weeks. Foreclosure must take place within 45–60 days of the initial notice. Borrower can file a *Notice of Intent to Cure* with the trustee at least fifteen days before the sale. The loan must be brought current by noon of the day before the sale.

Right of redemption: 75 days

Deficiency judgments: Allowed

Law

Title 38 Colorado Revised Statutes (Property Real and Personal) and Article 37 (Office of Public Trustee), Article 38 (Foreclosure Sales), Article 39 (Mortgages, Deeds of Trust

http://198.187.128.12/Colorado/lpext.dll?f=templates&fn=fs-main.htm&2.0

Resources

Consumer Protection: www.ago.state.co.us/consprot/CoResourceGuide.cfm

Division of Real Estate: www.dora.state.co.us/real-estate/index.htm

General: www.hud.gov/local/co/renting/tenantrights.cfm

Landlord/tenant law: www.bouldercolorado.gov/index.php?option=com_content&task=view&id=3767&Itemid=1406

Local HUD Information: www.hud.gov/local/index.cfm?state=co

University of Colorado: http://leeds.colorado.edu/realestate/index.aspx?id=295,247

Connecticut
Foreclosure laws
Judicial vs. nonjudicial: Judicial

Notice period: n/a

Right of redemption: Court decides

Deficiency judgments: Allowed, but there must be an appraisal process and hearing.

Law
Title 49 (Mortgages and Liens), Chapter 846 (Mortgages), §49-1 to §49-31j of the General Statutes of Connecticut

www.cga.ct.gov/2005/pub/Chap846.htm#Sec49-31e.htm

Resources
Consumer Protection: **www.ct.gov/dcp/site/default.asp**

Division of Real Estate and Real Estate Appraisal: **www.dora.state. co.us/real-estate**

Landlord/tenant law: **www.jud.ct.gov/faq/landlord.html**

Local HUD Information: **www.hud.gov/local/index.cfm?state=ct**

Residential Property Disclosure Form: **www.ct.gov/dcp/lib/ dcp/pdf/realestate_licensing_forms/disclose.pdf**

University of Connecticut: **www.business.uconn.edu/cms/cms/p266**

Delaware
Foreclosure laws
Judicial vs. nonjudicial: Judicial. Borrower has twenty days to respond to the complaint.

Notice period: Lis pendens notice is filed in the real estate records. Notice must be given fourteen days before the sale.

Typical time period for foreclosure: 175–200 days.

Right of redemption: Usually there is a confirmation hearing, scheduled with thirty days' notice after the sale. The borrower can redeem the property before this confirmation hearing, but not afterward.

Deficiency judgments: Allowed

Law
Delaware Code: Title 10 (Courts and Judicial Procedure), Part III Procedure, Chapter 49. Executions, Subchapter XI, Scire Facias on Mortgage

http://198.187.128.12/Delaware/lpext.dll?f=templates&fn=fs-main.htm&2.0

Resources
Consumer protection: http://attorneygeneral.delaware.gov

Disclosures: http://delcode.delaware.gov/title6/c025/sc07/index.shtml

General: www.hud.gov/local/de/renting/tenantrights.cfm

Landlord/tenant law: http://attorneygeneral.delaware.gov/consumers/protection/brochure/landlordcode.pdf

Local HUD Information: www.hud.gov/local/index.cfm?state=de

Real Estate Commission: http://dpr.delaware.gov/boards/realestate/index.shtml

District of Columbia
Foreclosure laws
Judicial vs. nonjudicial: Nonjudicial

Notice period: Notice of Sale must be sent to the borrower. *Notice of Sale* must also be sent to the mayor of the District of Columbia, at least thirty days prior to the sale, with the thirty-day time period to start running from the date of receipt of the notice.

Typical time period for foreclosure: 60 days

Right of redemption: None

Deficiency judgments: Allowed

Law
The laws that govern the foreclosure of *Deeds of Trust* are found in District of Columbia Code. A recent statute called the *Mortgage Foreclosure Procedures Reform Act*, was passed in 2002 and deals with predatory lending.

http://198.187.128.12/dc/lpext.dll?f=templates&fn=fs-main.htm& 2.0

Resources
Consumer Protection: **http://dcra.dc.gov/dcra/cwp/view,a,1343,q, 635148,dcraNav,7.7C334087.7C.asp**

Board of Real Estate: **http://dcra.dc.gov/dcra/cwp/view,a,1342,q, 600757.asp**

Fair Housing: **http://ohr.dc.gov/ohr/cwp/view,a,3,q,627574, ohrNav,%7C30953%7C.asp**

Landlord/tenant law:
http://dcra.dc.gov/dcra/frames.asp?doc=/dcra/lib/dcra/ information/forms_docs/pdf/tenantguide.pdf&group= 1697&open=%7C33466%7C

Local HUD Information: **www.hud.gov/local/index.cfm?state=dc**

Florida

Foreclosure laws

Judicial vs. nonjudicial: Judicial
Typical time period for foreclosure: 180–200 days
Right of redemption: None
Deficiency judgments: Allowed, except for a first mortgage purchase money loan on a borrower's principal residence.

Law

Florida Statutes 702.01 et. seq.
www.leg.state.fl.us

Resources

Consumer Protection: **http://myfloridalegal.com/consumer**
General: **www.hud.gov/local/fl/renting/tenantrights.cfm**
Landlord/tenant law: **www.800helpfla.com/landlord_text.html**
Local HUD Information: **www.hud.gov/local/index.cfm?state=fl**
Real Estate Commission: **www.myflorida.com/dbpr/re/
    frec_welcome.shtml**
Florida State University: **www.cob.fsu.edu/rmi/reecenter/
    ctr_ree.cfm**
University of Florida: **www.cba.ufl.edu/fire/realestate**

Georgia
Foreclosure laws

Judicial vs. nonjudicial: Nonjudicial is more common, but both are allowed.

Notice period: Lender must send a ten-day demand letter to the borrower. If not paid in that time, the lender must publish notice of foreclosure in the newspaper for four consecutive weeks.

Typical time period for foreclosure: 60–90 days

Right of redemption: None

Deficiency judgments: Allowed, but the lender must file suit within thirty days after the foreclosure.

Law

Georgia Code (O.C.G.A) O.C.G.A §44-14-162 et. seq. Actions to assert wrongful foreclosure for improper notice are referenced under O.C.G.A §9-11-65, and various notice requirements for sheriff's foreclosure sales are referenced under O.C.G.A. §9-13-140(a).

www.lawskills.com/code/ga/44/14/161/

Resources

Consumer Protection:
www.georgia.gov/00/channel_title/0,2094,4802_5041,00.html

Fair Housing: www.gceo.state.ga.us/housing.htm

General: www.hud.gov/local/ga/renting/tenantrights.cfm

Landlord/tenant law: www.dca.state.ga.us/housing/
HousingDevelopment/programs/downloads/landlord/
contents.html

Local HUD Information: www.hud.gov/local/index.cfm?state=ga

Real Estate Commission: www.grec.state.ga.us/

University of Georgia: www.terry.uga.edu/realestate/

Georgia State University: http://robinson.gsu.edu/realestate/rerc/index.html

Hawaii

Foreclosure laws

Judicial vs. nonjudicial: Both used equally.

Notice period: Newspaper notice must run for three consecutive weeks, with the last notice no less than fifteen days before the sale.

Typical time period for foreclosure: 60–90 days

Right of redemption: None, but the borrower may cure the default and reinstate the mortgage at any time up to three days before the foreclosure. The borrower must make the past due payments, plus costs and fees of the foreclosure.

Deficiency judgments: Allowed

Law

Chapter 667 et. seq., Hawaii Revised Statutes
www.capitol.Hawaii.gov

Resources

Consumer Protection: **www.hawaii.gov/dcca/areas/ocp**
Fair Housing: **www.hud.gov/local/hi/homeownership/fairhsg.cfm**
General: **www.hud.gov/local/hi/renting/tenantrights.cfm**
Landlord/tenant law: **www.hawaii.gov/dcca/areas/ocp/ landlord_tenant**
Local HUD Information: **www.hud.gov/local/index.cfm?state=hi**
Real Estate Branch: **www.hawaii.gov/hirec**

Idaho
Foreclosure laws

Judicial vs. nonjudicial: Both allowed, but nonjudicial foreclosures are more common.

Notice period: At least 120 days before the sale, a *Notice of Default* must be filed in the county in which the property is located. A copy of the notice must be published in the newspaper for four consecutive weeks, with the last notice published at least thirty days before the sale.

Right of redemption: None for nonjudicial foreclosures. For judicial foreclosures, the borrower can cure the default by paying all past due sums plus costs and expenses within 115 days of the recorded *Notice of Default.*

Deficiency judgments: Allowed, but the suit must be filed within ninety days of the foreclosure. The award cannot exceed the difference between the foreclosure sale price and the fair market value of the property.

Law

Title 45 Idaho Statutes (Liens, Mortgages and Pledges, Chapter 15 Trust Deeds) Section 45-1503 et. seq. Laws related to the postponement of foreclosure sales are found in Section 45-1506B.

http://www3.state.id.us/cgi-bin/newidst?sctid=450150003.K
http://www3.state.id.us/cgi-bin/newidst?sctid=450150006B.K

Resources

Consumer Protection: http://www2.state.id.us/ag/consumer/
Disclosures: http://www3.state.id.us/idstat/TOC/55025KTOC.html
Fair Housing: www.ihfa.org/research_fairhousing.asp
General: www.hud.gov/local/id/renting/tenantrights.cfm

Landlord/tenant law: **http://www2.state.id.us/ag/consumer/tips/ LandlordTenant.pdf**

Local HUD Information: **www.hud.gov/local/index.cfm?state=ia**

Real Estate Commission: **www.idahorealestatecommission.com**

Illinois
Foreclosure laws
Judicial vs. nonjudicial: Judicial

Notice period: Borrowers can reinstate the mortgage within ninety days of personal service of the foreclosure lawsuit.

Typical time period for foreclosure: 215 days

Right of redemption: On residential properties, the redemptory period is seven months from the date the foreclosure suit is filed or three months from the date the final order of foreclosure is entered. A foreclosure sale cannot occur until these time limits expire. Reinstatement and redemption rights can be exercised only once every five years. There is no postsale right of redemption.

Deficiency judgments: Allowed

Law
735 ILCS 5/Art XV

www.ilga.gov/legislation/ilcs/ilcs2.asp?ChapterID=56

Resources
Consumer Protection: www.illinoisattorneygeneral.gov/consumers/index.html

Disclosures: www.illinoisrealtor.org/iar/buy_sell/legal/disclosure.html

Fair Housing: www.state.il.us/dhr/Housenet/index.html

Landlord/tenant law: www.hud.gov/local/il/renting/tenantrights.cfm www.chicityclerk.com/legislation/codes/chapter5_12.pdf

Local HUD Information: www.hud.gov/local/index.cfm?state=il

Bureau of Real Estate Professions: ww.idfpr.com/dpr/RE/realmain.asp

DePaul University: http://realestate.depaul.edu/index.htm

University of Illinois: www.business.uiuc.edu/orer

Northwestern University: www.kellogg.northwestern.edu/academic/realestate/index.htm

Indiana
Foreclosure laws
Judicial vs. nonjudicial: Judicial

Notice period: Lender usually must wait three months to execute on an order of foreclosure. When the order is entered, the sheriff must publish the notice in the newspaper once a week for three consecutive weeks. The first notice must be at least thirty days before the proposed sale. The borrower must be personally served with a notice of the sale.

Typical time period for foreclosure: 150–200 days

Right of redemption: Presale right of redemption, after the foreclosure order has been entered but before the sale takes place. There is no postforeclosure right of redemption.

Deficiency judgments: Allowed

Law
Indiana Code, Article 29 (Mortgages), Chapter 7 (Foreclosure, Redemption, Sale, Right to Retain Possession)
www.in.gov/legislative/ic/code/title32/ar29/ch7.html

Resources
Consumer Protection: **www.in.gov/attorneygeneral/consumer**
Disclosures: **www.in.gov/icpr/webfile/formsdiv/46234.pdf**
Fair Housing: **www.in.gov/icrc/fairhousing**
Landlord/tenant law: **www.hud.gov/local/in/renting/tenantrights.cfm**
Local HUD Information: **www.hud.gov/local/index.cfm?state=in**
Real Estate Commission: **www.in.gov/pla/bandc/estate**
University of Indiana: **www.indiana.edu/~cres/realestate**

Iowa
Foreclosure laws
Judicial vs. nonjudicial: Judicial

Notice period: Borrowers generally have the right to cure within thirty days after receiving the default notice.

Typical time period for foreclosure: 150–180 days

Right of redemption: One year for homestead property. This can be shortened to six months if the lender gives up the right to a deficiency judgment, and it can be shortened to sixty days if the property is abandoned.

Deficiency judgments: Allowed unless waived.

Law
Chapter 654 of Iowa Code (Foreclosure of Real Estate Mortgages). Other pertinent laws are found in Chapter 615 and Chapter 628 (Redemption).
www.legis.state.ia.us/IACODE/2003SUPPLEMENT/654/

Resources
Consumer Protection: www.state.ia.us/government/ag
Disclosures: www.legis.state.ia.us/IACODE/2003/558A
Fair Housing: www.iowarealtors.com/consumers/equal.htm
Landlord/tenant law: www.hud.gov/local/ia/renting/tenantrights.cfm
Local HUD Information: www.hud.gov/local/index.cfm?state=ia
Real Estate Commission: www.state.ia.us/government/com/prof/sales/home.html

Kansas

Foreclosure laws

Judicial vs. nonjudicial: Judicial

Notice period: Notice of sale must be published for three consecutive weeks, with the last notice published no more than fourteen days and no less than seven days prior to the sale.

Typical time period for foreclosure: 120–140 days

Right of redemption: One year, but this can be shortened by the court if it finds the property has been abandoned. Right of redemption can also be waived in the loan documents, but not for residential or agricultural property.

Deficiency judgments: Allowed

Law

Kansas Statutes Annotated (K.S.A.), Chapter 60, Article 24 (2410) (Executions and Orders of Sale)

www.kslegislature.org/legsrv-statutes/getStatute.do?number=23277

Resources

Consumer Protection: www.ksag.org/content/page/id/39

Disclosures: www.kansasrealtor.com/secure/contracts/residential/propdisc.pdf

Fair Housing: www.khrc.net

Landlord/tenant law: www.hud.gov/local/ks/renting/tenantrights.cfm

Local HUD Information: www.hud.gov/local/index.cfm?state=ks

Real Estate Commission: www.accesskansas.org/krec

Wichita State University: http://realestate.wichita.edu/research.asp

Kentucky
Foreclosure laws
Judicial vs. nonjudicial: Judicial

Notice period: The lender must advertise the sale for three weeks.

Typical time period for foreclosure: 150 days

Right of redemption: Limited postsale right of redemption for one year, but only if the sale price is less than two-thirds of the appraised value of the property. The right of redemption can be sold to others.

Deficiency judgments: Allowed

Law
Kentucky Revised Statutes (KRS) Chapter 426 (Enforcement of Judgments)

www.lrc.ky.gov/KRS/426-00/CHAPTER.HTM

Resources
Consumer Protection:
www.kentucky.gov/Portal/Category/hea_consumer

Disclosures: www.lrc.state.ky.us/kar/201/011/350.htm

Fair Housing: www.kyhousing.org

Landlord/tenant law: www.hud.gov/local/ky/renting/tenantrights.cfm

Local HUD Information: www.hud.gov/local/index.cfm?state=ky

Real Estate Commission: www.krec.ky.gov

University of Kentucky: http://gatton.uky.edu/CRES/Index.html

Louisiana

Foreclosure laws

Judicial vs. nonjudicial: Judicial

Notice period: Under the *executory process* the borrower generally receives a three-day notice of default. The lender must advertise the sale once a week for thirty days before the sale.

Typical time period for foreclosure: Ordinary process takes 180–270 days to complete. *Executory process*, which is available as a result of a pre-signed confession of judgment, can be completed within six months.

Right of redemption: None

Deficiency judgments: Allowed

Law

Louisiana Revised Statutes, Title 10:9-629
www.legis.state.la.us/lss/lss.asp?doc=74514

Resources

Consumer Protection:
   www.ag.state.la.us/ConsumerProtection.aspx
Disclosures: www.lrec.state.la.us/forms.htm#residential
Fair Housing: www.lafairhousing.org
Landlord/tenant law: www.ag.state.la.us/publications/landlord.htm
Local HUD Information: www.hud.gov/local/index.cfm?state=la
Real Estate Commission: www.lrec.state.la.us
Louisiana State University: www.bus.lsu.edu/centers/reri

Maine
Foreclosure laws

Judicial vs. nonjudicial: Judicial, although nonjudicial foreclosure is allowed for nonresidential properties.

Notice period: Sale must be advertised for three consecutive weeks.

Typical time period for foreclosure: 180–200 days

Right of redemption: One year or three months, depending on when the mortgage was executed. The right of redemption must expire before certain steps can be taken to complete the foreclosure sale.

Deficiency judgments: Allowed, but limited by the fair market value of the property as appraised at the time of the foreclosure.

Law

Maine Revised Statutes, Title 14, part 4, Chapter 403 (Title to Real Estate by Levy and Execution). Power of sale provisions related to nonresidential mortgages is found in Title 33 (Mortgages of Real Property), Chapter 9, §501-§553A.

http://janus.state.me.us/legis/statutes/14/title14ch403sec0.html

http://janus.state.me.us/legis/statutes/33/title33ch9sec0.html

Resources

Consumer Protection: www.maine.gov/ag/?r=protection

Disclosures: http://janus.state.me.us/legis/statutes/33/title33sec173.html

Fair Housing: www.maine.gov/mhrc/publications/fair_housing.html

Landlord/tenant law: www.hud.gov/local/me/renting/tenantrights.cfm

Local HUD Information: www.hud.gov/local/index.cfm?state=me

Real Estate Commission: www.maine.gov/pfr/professionallicensing/index.shtml

University of Southern Maine: http://cree.usm.maine.edu

Maryland
Foreclosure laws
Judicial vs. nonjudicial: Judicial
Typical time period for foreclosure: 90–100 days
Right of redemption: Court decides redemptory period.
Deficiency judgments: Allowed

Law
Maryland Rules, Title 14 (Sales of Property), Chapter 200 (Foreclosure of lien instruments)

Resources
Consumer Protection: **www.oag.state.md.us/Consumer/index.htm**
Disclosures: **www.dllr.state.md.us/forms/danddform.doc**
Fair Housing: **www.mchr.state.md.us**
Landlord/tenant law: **www.hud.gov/local/md/renting/tenantrights.cfm**
Local HUD Information: **www.hud.gov/local/index.cfm?state=md**
Real Estate Commission: **www.dllr.state.md.us/license/occprof/recomm.html**

Massachusetts
Foreclosure laws

Judicial vs. nonjudicial: Nonjudicial is more common, but judicial foreclosure is permitted.

Notice period: Notice of sale must be recorded in the county where the property is located. Notice of sale must be served on the borrower at least fourteen days before the sale date. Newspaper notice must run for three consecutive weeks.

Typical time period for foreclosure: 75–90 days

Right of redemption: None, unless the lender attempts to obtain a deficiency judgment under certain circumstances.

Deficiency judgments: Generally not allowed.

Law

Chapter 244 of the General Laws of Massachusetts
www.mass.gov/legis/laws/mgl/gl-244-toc.htm

Resources

Consumer Protection: **www.ago.state.ma.us**
Disclosures: **www.mass.gov/legis/laws/mgl/111-197a.htm**
Fair Housing: **www.massfairhousing.org/joomla/index.php? option=com_wrapper&Itemid=36**
Landlord/tenant law: **www.hud.gov/local/ma/renting/tenantrights.cfm**
Local HUD Information: **www.hud.gov/local/index.cfm?state=ma**
Real Estate Commission: **www.mass.gov**
Harvard University: **www.jchs.harvard.edu**
Massachusetts Institute of Technology: **http://web.mit.edu/cre/ index.html**

Michigan
Foreclosure laws
Judicial vs. nonjudicial: Nonjudicial usually, but judicial foreclosure is allowed.

Notice period: Publication for four consecutive weeks before the sale.

Typical time period for foreclosure: 60 days

Right of redemption: Six months if the property is residential, does not exceed four units, and the default amount is more than two-thirds of the original loan amount. Thirty days if the property has been abandoned. In all other cases, the redemption period is one year.

Deficiency judgments: Allowed

Law
Chapter 451 of Michigan Compiled Laws
www.legislature.mi.gov

Resources
Consumer Protection: www.michigan.gov/ag/0,1607,7-164-17334_ 17362—,00.html

Disclosures: http://law.justia.com/michigan/codes/mcl-chap565/ mcl-act-92-of-1993.html

Fair Housing: www.fairhousinginmichigan.org/joomla

Landlord/tenant law: www.hud.gov/local/mi/renting/tenantrights.cfm

Local HUD Information: www.hud.gov/local/index.cfm?state=mi

Real Estate Commission: www.michigan.gov/cis/0,1607,7-154- 35299_35414_35475-114980—,00.html

Forms located at: www.cis.state.mi.us/dms/results.asp?docowner= BCSC&doccat=Real+Estate&Search=Search

Real Estate Law Book: www.michigan.gov/documents/cis/redbook_ revised_February_2007-1_187962_7.pdf

Minnesota
Foreclosure laws

Judicial vs. Nonjudicial: Nonjudicial is more common.

Notice period: The attorney who will conduct the foreclosure must file a *Power of Attorney* in the real estate records. He or she must also publish a notice in the newspaper for six consecutive weeks. Notice must be served on all owners and occupants at least four weeks before the sale. For homestead property, the notice must be served at least eight weeks before the sale.

Typical time period for foreclosure: 120 days

Right of redemption: Six months, unless the amount due is less than two-thirds of the original loan amount and the property exceeds ten acres, or unless the property exceeds forty acres, in which case the redemption period is one year. For mortgages signed after 12/31/89, the redemption period can be shortened to thirty days by a court if the property has been abandoned.

Deficiency judgments: Allowed, but limited to the difference between the fair market value of the property and the foreclosure sale price.

Law

Minnesota Statutes, Chapter 580.01 et. seq. (nonjudicial foreclosures)

Minnesota Statutes (2004) Chapter 581.01 et. seq. (Foreclosure by Action)

www.revisor.leg.state.mn.us/stats/580

www.revisor.leg.state.mn.us/stats/581

Resources

Consumer Protection: **www.ag.state.mn.us**

Disclosures: **www.mnrealtor.com/forms/faq/asis.html**

Fair Housing: **www.mnhousing.gov/about/fairhousing/index.aspx**

Landlord/tenant law: **www.hud.gov/local/mn/renting/tenantrights. cfm**

Local HUD Information: **www.hud.gov/local/index.cfm?state=mn**
Department of Commerce (Real Estate):
**www.state.mn.us/portal/mn/jsp/content.do?subchannel=-536881389
&id=-536881352&agency=Commerce**

Mississippi
Foreclosure laws

Judicial vs. nonjudicial: Nonjudicial is more common.

Notice period: A *Notice of Sale* must be recorded in the real estate records. A *Notice of Foreclosure Sale* must be published in the newspaper for three consecutive weeks.

Typical time period for foreclosure: 60–90 days

Right of redemption: Six months after sale

Deficiency judgments: Allowed

Law

Foreclosure sales: Title 11 (Civil Practice and Procedure) §11-5-93 et. seq. Other provisions, including rights of redemption: §15-1-19 and §15-1-21

http://198.187.128.12/Mississippi/lpext.dll?f=templates&fn=fs-main.htm&2.0

Resources

Consumer Protection: www.ago.state.ms.us/divisions/consumer

Disclosures: www.mrec.state.ms.us/docs/mrec_forms_property_condition_disclosure.pdf

Fair Housing: www.msbar.org/10_you_and_your_home.php?spot=1199&archive=19

Landlord/tenant law: www.hud.gov/local/ms/renting/tenantrights.cfm

Local HUD Information: www.hud.gov/local/index.cfm?state=ms

Real Estate Commission: www.mrec.state.ms.us/

Missouri
Foreclosure laws
Judicial vs. nonjudicial: Nonjudicial is more common.

Notice period: Notice of foreclosure must be published at least twenty times and continue up to the day of the sale if the property is located in a city of 50,000 or more persons. If not, then the notice must be published for four consecutive weeks, with the last notice published no more than one week from the date of sale.

Typical time period for foreclosure: 60–90 days

Right of redemption: One year for judicial foreclosures, but the borrower must give notice of intent to redeem within twenty days of the sale and must post a bond in the amount of all costs and fees, not including the loan principal and interest.

Deficiency judgments: Not allowed

Law
Chapter 443.327 Missouri Revised Statutes
www.moga.state.mo.us/STATUTES/C443.HTM

Resources
Consumer Protection: www.ago.mo.gov/divisions/
consumerprotection.htm

Fair Housing: www.moga.mo.gov/statutes/c200-299/2130000040.htm

Landlord/tenant law: www.hud.gov/local/mo/renting/tenantrights.cfm

Local HUD Information: www.hud.gov/local/index.cfm?state=mo

Real Estate Commission: http://pr.mo.gov/realestate.asp

Montana
Foreclosure laws
Judicial vs. nonjudicial: Nonjudicial is more common.

Notice period: Lender must record a *Notice of Sale* at least 120 days prior to the sale and serve a copy of that notice on the borrower by certified or registered mail. Newspaper notice must be published once a week for three weeks.

Typical time period for foreclosure: 140–150 days

Right of redemption: None for nonjudicial foreclosures.

Deficiency judgments: Not allowed after a nonjudicial foreclosure.

Law
Montana Code Annotated (2003) Section 71-1-101 et. seq.
http://data.opi.state.mt.us/bills/mca/71/1/71-1-101.htm

Resources
Consumer Protection: **www.doj.mt.gov/consumer**
Disclosures: **http://data.opi.state.mt.us/bills/mca/75/3/75-3-606.htm**
Fair Housing: **www.fairhousing.montana.com**
Landlord/tenant law: **www.hud.gov/local/mt/renting/tenantrights.cfm**
Local HUD Information: **www.hud.gov/local/index.cfm?state=mt**
Board of Realty Regulation: **http://commerce.state.mt.us/**

Nebraska
Foreclosure laws

Judicial vs. nonjudicial: Both allowed, but nonjudicial foreclosure is more common.

Notice period: Lender must file a *Notice of Default* and *Notice of Sale* in the deed records where the property is located. Not less than ten days later, a copy must be served on the borrower and any junior lienholders. A *Notice of Foreclosure Sale*—which is usually incorporated into the *Notice of Default*—must be sent to the borrower and all interested parties at least twenty days prior to the sale. A notice of sale must be published for five consecutive weeks, with the last publication date at least ten days prior to the sale.

Typical time period for foreclosure: 90–120 days

Right of redemption: None for nonjudicial foreclosures

Deficiency judgments: Allowed, but limited to the difference between the foreclosure sale price and the fair market value of the property.

Law

Chapter 76, Nebraska Statutes
http://uniweb.legislature.ne.gov/legaldocs/search.php

Resources

Consumer Protection: www.ago.state.ne.us/consumer/
Disclosures: www.sos.state.ne.us/rules-and-regs/regsearch/Rules/
  Real_Estate_Commission/Title-302/Chapter-1.pdf
Fair Housing: www.neoc.ne.gov/laws/hsng.htm
Landlord/tenant law: www.hud.gov/local/ne/renting/tenantrights.cfm
Local HUD Information: www.hud.gov/local/index.cfm?state=ne
Real Estate Commission: www.nrec.state.ne.us

Nevada
Foreclosure laws
Judicial vs. nonjudicial: Nonjudicial is more common.

Notice period: Lender must give borrower 35-day notice of default and an opportunity to cure. A *Notice of Default* must be filed in the real estate records at least three months prior to the sale. Newspaper notice must be published for three consecutive weeks. Borrower may cure any time after receiving the notice and up to fifteen days before the sale by filing an *Intent to Cure* with the public trustee's office.

Typical time period for foreclosure: 120 days

Right of redemption: One year after judicial foreclosures.

Deficiency judgments: Allowed

Law
Chapter 106, Nevada Revised Statutes
www.leg.state.nv.us/nrs/NRS-107.html
www.leg.state.nv.us/nrs/ NRS-106.html

Resources
Consumer Protection: **http://ag.state.nv.us/org/bcp/bcp.htm**
Disclosures: **http://red.state.nv.us/forms/547.pdf**
Fair Housing: **www.nfhc.org**
Landlord/tenant law: **www.hud.gov/local/nv/renting/tenantrights.cfm**
Local HUD Information: **www.hud.gov/local/index.cfm?state=nv**
Real Estate Division: **www.red.state.nv.us**

New Hampshire

Foreclosure laws

Judicial vs. nonjudicial: Nonjudicial

Notice period: Notice of sale must be recorded in the real estate records and sent to the borrower at least 25 days prior to the sale. A copy of the notice must then be published in the newspaper for three consecutive weeks.

Typical time period for foreclosure: 60–70 days

Right of redemption: None

Deficiency judgments: Allowed

Law

Title 38 New Hampshire Revised Statutes, Chapter 479 (Mortgages of Realty).

www.gencourt.state.nh.us/ie/

Resources

Consumer Protection: **http://doj.nh.gov/consumer/**

Disclosures: **www.nh.gov/nhrec/adrule2f.html#rea701**

Fair Housing: **www.nhla.org/nhlafhp.php**

Landlord/tenant law: **www.hud.gov/local/nh/renting/tenantrights.cfm**

Local HUD Information: **www.hud.gov/local/index.cfm?state=nh**

Real Estate Commission: **www.nh.gov/nhrec**

New Jersey
Foreclosure laws
Judicial vs. nonjudicial: Judicial

Typical time period for foreclosure: 250 days

Right of redemption: 10 days after the sale

Deficiency judgments: Allowed, but the borrower must be given credit for the fair market value of the property, no matter what the sale price was.

Law
N.J.S.A. 2A:50-1 et. seq.

http://lis.njleg.state.nj.us/

Resources
Consumer Protection: www.njconsumeraffairs.gov/ocp.htm

Disclosures: www.betterhomesnj.com/pdf/SELLERS_
    PROPERTY_CONDITION_DISCLOSURE_STATEMENT.pdf

Fair Housing: www.state.nj.us/dca/fairhousing

Landlord/tenant law: www.hud.gov/local/nj/renting/tenantrights.cfm

Local HUD Information: www.hud.gov/local/index.cfm?state=nj

Real Estate Commission: www.state.nj.us/dobi/remnu.shtml

New Mexico
Foreclosure laws
Judicial vs. nonjudicial: Judicial is more common, but nonjudicial fore-closure is allowed for commercial loans in excess of $500,000, and certain other instances involving low-income housing.

Notice period: Notice of sale must be published for four weeks before the sale, and it generally takes four months after entry of the order for sale before the sale can actually take place.

Typical time period for foreclosure: 120–180 days

Right of redemption: 9 months

Deficiency judgments: Allowed except in the case of low-income housing.

Law
New Mexico Statutes Annotated (1978); Chapter 48, Articles 48-7-1 to 48-7-24

www.conwaygreene.com

Resources
Consumer Protection: **www.ago.state.nm.us/divs/cons/cons.htm**

Disclosures: HUD-required disclosures, such as those for lead-based paint

Landlord/tenant law: **www.thelpa.com/lpa/landlord-tenant-law/new-mexico-landlord-tenant-law.html**

Local HUD Information: **www.hud.gov/local/index.cfm?state=nm**

Real Estate Commission: **www.rld.state.nm.us/Real_Estate_Commission/index.html**

New York
Foreclosure laws

Judicial vs. nonjudicial: Judicial, but nonjudicial foreclosure is allowed in limited circumstances.

Notice period: Notice of sale must be published for four weeks, usually not commencing until four months after entry of the order authorizing the foreclosure sale.

Typical time period for foreclosure: 120–180 days

Right of redemption: None

Deficiency judgments: Allowed, but the creditor must file a motion within ninety days after the foreclosure sale.

Law

New York State Consolidated Laws, Article 13
http://assembly.state.ny.us

Resources

Consumer Protection: www.oag.state.ny.us/consumer/consumer_issues.html

Disclosures: www.dos.state.ny.us/lcns/pdfs/1614.pdf

Fair Housing: www.dhcr.state.ny.us/fheo/fheo.htm

Landlord/tenant law: www.hud.gov/local/ny/renting/tenantrights.cfm

Local HUD Information: www.hud.gov/local/index.cfm?state=ny

Office of Real Property Services: www.orps.state.ny.us

Cornell University: http://realestate.cornell.edu/

New York University: www.law.nyu.edu/realestatecenter

North Carolina
Foreclosure laws
Judicial vs. nonjudicial: Nonjudicial is more common.

Notice period: Notice must be given to the borrower at least twenty days before the sale. Notice must be published in the newspaper for two consecutive weeks.

Right of redemption: There is a ten-day postforeclosure redemption period, during which time anyone can pay an upset bid price of 5% more than the sale price and buy the property.

Deficiency judgments: Allowed, but the borrower can defend against it with proof of the fair market value of the property.

Law
North Carolina General Statutes, Chapter 45 (Mortgages and Deeds of Trust), Article 2, Article 2A as referenced in §45-4 to §45-21.38

www.ncga.state.nc.us/gascripts/Statutes/StatutesTOC.pl?Chapter=0045

Resources
Consumer Protection:
www.ncdoj.com/consumerprotection/cp_about.jsp

Disclosures: www.ncrec.state.nc.us/forms/rec422.pdf

Fair Housing: www.ncruralcenter.org/guidebook/viewresource.asp?ID=138

Landlord/tenant law: www.hud.gov/local/nc/renting/tenantrights.cfm

Local HUD Information: www.hud.gov/local/index.cfm?state=nc

Real Estate Commission: www.ncrec.state.nc.us/default.html

University of North Carolina: www.kenan-flagler.unc.edu/KI/realEstate/research.cfm

North Dakota
Foreclosure laws
Judicial vs. nonjudicial: Judicial

Notice period: Notice must be given to borrower at least thirty days prior to the action being filed, advising that foreclosure will occur if the default is not cured within thirty days.

Typical time period for foreclosure: 90 days

Right of redemption: Sixty days for most properties. Agricultural property has a one-year right of redemption.

Deficiency judgments: Not allowed for residential properties with up to four units and forty contiguous acres. For agriculture property, the deficiency is measured by the difference between the fair market value of the property and the debt owed.

Law
2005 North Dakota Century Code Chapter 32-19-01 et. seq. **www.legis.nd.gov/cencode/t32.html**

Resources
Consumer Protection: **www.ag.state.nd.us/CPAT/CPAT.htm**

Fair Housing: **www.ndfhc.org**

Landlord/tenant law: **www.hud.gov/local/nd/renting/tenantrights.cfm**
www.ag.state.nd.us/Brochures/FactSheet/TenantRights.pdf

Local HUD Information: **www.hud.gov/local/index.cfm?state=nd**

Real Estate Commission: **www.governor.state.nd.us/boards/boards-query.asp?Board_ID=93**

Ohio

Foreclosure laws

Judicial vs. nonjudicial: Judicial

Notice period: Must be advertised for thirty days prior to the sale by running newspaper notices once a week for three consecutive weeks.

Typical time period for foreclosure: 120–180 days

Right of redemption: Borrower can redeem the property after the sale but before the judicial confirmation of the sale.

Deficiency judgments: Allowed

Law

§2323.07 of Ohio Revised Code.
http://codes.ohio.gov/orc/2323.07

Resources

Consumer Protection: www.ag.state.oh.us

Disclosures: www.com.state.oh.us/real/documents/respropdisclform. eff2007-01-01.pdf

Fair Housing: http://cohhio.org/

Foreclosure Prevention Task Force—Governor's Office: www.com. state.oh.us/admn/foreclosure_links.aspx

Landlord/tenant law: www.ohiolegalservices.org/OSLSA/PublicWeb/ Library/Index/1690000/1630100/index_html

Local HUD Information: www.hud.gov/local/index.cfm?state=oh

Division of Real Estate and Professional Licensing: www.com. state.oh.us/real

University of Cincinnati: www.business.uc.edu/realestate

Ohio State University: http://fisher.osu.edu/realestate/index.html

Oklahoma
Foreclosure laws
Judicial vs. nonjudicial: Nonjudicial is more common.

Notice period: Lender must send borrower 35-day *Notice of Default* and *Opportunity to Cure.* If the borrower has been in default three times in the last 24 months, no additional notice is required. If the property is homestead property, the borrower gets four chances—within 24 months—for default notice and opportunity to cure. Once the borrower has exhausted his or her cure rights, the lender can accelerate foreclosure without additional notice. Notice of the sale must be published in a newspaper once a week for four consecutive weeks, with the first notice published no less than thirty days prior to the sale.

Right of redemption: None

Deficiency judgments: Allowed, but limited by the difference between the fair market value of the property and the debt.

Law
Title 46 Oklahoma Statutes (Oklahoma Power of sale Mortgage Foreclosure Act) Chapter 2A §43

www.oscn.net/applications/oscn/deliverdocument.asp?citeID=72061

Resources
Disclosures: www.okbar.org/obj/articles_04/051504shelton.htm
www.state.ok.us/~orec/news.html
Fair Housing: www.ohc.ok.gov/housing/housing.htm
www.hud.gov/offices/fheo/FHLaws/index.cfm
Landlord/tenant law: www.hud.gov/local/ok/renting/tenantrights.cfm
Local HUD Information: www.hud.gov/local/index.cfm?state=ok
Real Estate Commission: www.ok.gov/OREC

Real Estate Contract Form Approved by the Oklahoma Real Estate Commission: **http://ok.gov/OREC/documents/Uniform%20Contract%20of%20Sale%20of%20Real%20Estate.(Field)pdf.pdf**

Oregon
Foreclosure laws

Judicial vs. nonjudicial: Nonjudicial is more common.

Notice period: A *Notice of Default* must be filed in the real estate records, and the borrower must receive a copy of the *Notice of Default* at least 120 days before the sale date. Notice of the sale must be published once a week in the newspaper for four consecutive weeks, with the last notice at least twenty days prior to sale. There is a thirty-day publication period requirement.

Right of redemption: 180 days. Must be exercised by giving notice to the sheriff no more than thirty days and no less than two days before redemption.

Deficiency judgments: Allowed

Law

Chapter 86 Oregon Revised Statutes (Mortgages; Trust Deeds) and Chapter 88 (Foreclosure of Mortgages and Other Liens)
www.leg.state.or.us/ors/086.html
www.leg.state.or.us/ors/088.html

Resources

Consumer Protection: **www.doj.state.or.us/finfraud**
Disclosures: **www.osbar.org/public/legalinfo/1201.htm**
www.leg.state.or.us/ors/105.html (you must then scroll down to 105.464)
Fair Housing: **www.fhco.org/**
Landlord/tenant law: **www.hud.gov/local/or/renting/tenantrights.cfm**
Local HUD Information: **www.hud.gov/local/index.cfm?state=or**
Real Estate Agency: **www.oregon.gov/REA/index.shtml**

Pennsylvania
Foreclosure laws
Judicial vs. nonjudicial: Judicial

Notice period: Notice of intent to foreclose must be sent sixty days prior to taking a default judgment after the foreclosure suit has been filed if the borrower has not answered. The borrower will usually have thirty days after that to set up a payment plan or cure the default during that time period.

Typical time period for a foreclosure: 120 days

Right of redemption: None

Deficiency judgments: Allowed

Law
Pa. R.C.P. 1141-1164 (Actions to Foreclose a Mortgage), 3180-3183 (Judgments in Mortgage Foreclosure), and 8103 et. seq. (Deficiency Judgments) (these are civil procedure rules). The Loan Interest & Protection Law, 41 P.S. §101 et. seq. (Act 6) and the Homeowners Emergency Assistance Act, 35 P.S. § 1680.401 et. seq. (Act 91) are the statutory references.
www.pacode.com/secure/data/231/chapter1000/subchapItoc.html
http://members.aol.com/DKM1/41.Cp.4.html

Resources
Consumer Protection: www.attorneygeneral.gov

Disclosures: www.dos.state.pa.us/bpoa/lib/bpoa/20/real_estate_comm/sellers_property_disclosure_statement.pdf

Fair Housing: www.phrc.state.pa.us

Landlord/tenant law: www.hud.gov/local/pa/renting/tenantrights.cfm

Local HUD Information: www.hud.gov/local/index.cfm?state=pa

Real Estate Commission: **www.dos.state.pa.us/bpoa/cwp/view. asp?a=1104&q=433107&papowerNavDLTEST=%7C30600% 7C30609%7C30610%7C**

Pennsylvania State University: **www.smeal.psu.edu/ires**

University of Pennsylvania: **http://realestate.wharton.upenn.edu/**

Puerto Rico

Foreclosure laws

Judicial vs. nonjudicial: Judicial
Typical time period for foreclosure: 60–90 days
Right of redemption: None
Deficiency judgments: Allowed

Law

Puerto Rico Civil Code, Title 31 §1291h
Puerto Rico Civil Code, Title 31 §1291h.
http://nersp.nerdc.ufl.edu/~malavet/seminar/prcodein.htm

Resources

Fair Housing: **www.hud.gov/local/pr-vi/working/localpo/fheo.cfm**
Local HUD Information: **www.hud.gov/local/index.cfm?state=pr-vi**

Rhode Island
Foreclosure laws
Judicial vs. nonjudicial: Judicial
Typical time period for foreclosure: 60–80 days
Right of redemption: None
Deficiency judgments: Allowed

Law
State of Rhode Island General Laws, Title 34 (Property), Chapter
  34-27 (Mortgage Foreclosure and Sale)
www.rilin.state.ri.us/Statutes/TITLE34/INDEX.HTM

Resources
Consumer Protection: **www.riag.state.ri.us/civil/unit.php?name=**
  consumer
Disclosures: **www.rilin.state.ri.us/statutes/TITLE5/5-20.8/**
  5-20.8-2.HTM
Fair Housing: **www.rifairhousing.org**
Landlord/tenant laws:
  www.hud.gov/local/ri/renting/tenantrights.cfm
Local HUD Information: **www.hud.gov/local/index.cfm?state=ri**
Real Estate Commission: **www.dbr.state.ri.us/divisions/**
  commlicensing/realestate.php

South Carolina
Foreclosure laws
Judicial vs. nonjudicial: Judicial

Notice period: Borrower must receive notice of sale, which must also be published in the newspaper once a week for three consecutive weeks.

Typical time period for foreclosure: 150–180 days

Right of redemption: None

Deficiency judgments: Allowed, but if the lender seeks a deficiency judgment, the borrower may apply for an appraisal. The value of the appraisal will be substituted for the sale amount.

Law
South Carolina Code of Laws (2004) Title 29 (Mortgages and Other Liens), Chapter 3, Article 7 (Foreclosures) (Section 29-3-610 et. seq.).

www.scstatehouse.net/code/t29c003.htm

Resources
Consumer Protection: **www.scconsumer.gov**

Disclosures: **www.llr.state.sc.us/POL/REC/RECPDF/DOC360.pdf**

Fair Housing: **www.state.sc.us/schac/summary_of_the_south_ carolina_fa.htm**

Landlord/tenant laws:
   www.hud.gov/local/sc/renting/tenantrights.cfm

Local HUD Information: **www.hud.gov/local/index.cfm?state=sc**

Real Estate Commission: **www.llr.state.sc.us/POL/REC**

University of South Carolina: **http://mooreschool.sc.edu/moore/ sccre/**

South Dakota

Foreclosure laws

Judicial vs. nonjudicial: Both, but judicial is more common.

Notice period: Notice must be published in a local newspaper. At least twenty-one days before the sale, the lender must deliver a written copy of the sale notice to the borrower.

Typical time period for foreclosure: 150 days

Right of redemption: Six months, unless property is vacant, in which case redemption period is two months.

Resources

Consumer Protection: **www.state.sd.us/attorney/office/divisions/consumer/**

Disclosures: **http://legis.state.sd.us/statutes/DisplayStatute.aspx?Type=Statute&Statute=43-4-44**

Fair Housing: **www.ndfhc.org/**

Landlord/tenant: **www.hud.gov/local/sd/renting/tenantrights.cfm**

Local HUD Information: **www.hud.gov/local/index.cfm?state=sd**

Real Estate Commission: **www.state.sd.us/sdrec**

Tennessee

Foreclosure laws

Judicial vs. nonjudicial: Nonjudicial is more common, but judicial foreclosures are allowed.

Notice period: Must be published in the newspaper once a week for three consecutive weeks, with the first notice at least twenty days before the sale. Borrowers may reinstate their loan up until the date of the sale by paying all sums due, plus cost of collection.

Right of redemption: Two years, unless the right has been waived in the loan documents.

Deficiency judgments: Allowed

Resources

Consumer Protection: **www.state.tn.us/consumer**

Disclosures: **http://michie.lexisnexis.com/tennessee/lpext.dll?f= templates&fn=main-h.htm&cp=**

Fair Housing: **www.tennfairhousing.org**

Landlord/tenant law: **www.hud.gov/local/tn/renting/tenantrights.cfm**

Local HUD Information: **www.hud.gov/local/index.cfm?state=tn**

Real Estate Commission: **www.state.tn.us/commerce/boards/trec**

Texas
Foreclosure laws
Judicial vs. nonjudicial: Nonjudicial

Notice period: Borrower must receive a twenty-day demand letter to cure the default and bring the loan current. After the twenty days have expired, and at least twenty-one days before the sale, the creditor must file a *Notice of Foreclosure* with the county recorder and send a copy to the borrower.

Right of redemption: None

Deficiency judgments: Limited to the difference between the foreclosure sale price and the appraised fair market value of the property.

Law
Title 5, Chapter 51 of Texas Code.
http://tlo2.tlc.state.tx.us/statutes/pr.toc.htm

Resources
Consumer Protection: **www.oag.state.tx.us/consumer/consumer.shtml**

Disclosures: **www.trec.state.tx.us/pdf/contracts/OP-H.pdf**

Fair Housing: **www.twc.state.tx.us/crd/housing_fact.html**

Landlord/tenant law: **http://studentlife.tamu.edu/scrs/sls/SelfHelp/tenant.htm**

Local HUD Information: **www.hud.gov/local/index.cfm?state=tx**

Real Estate Commission: **www.trec.state.tx.us**

Southern Methodist University: **www.cox.smu.edu/centers/realestate**

Texas A&M University: **http://recenter.tamu.edu/**

Utah

Foreclosure laws

Judicial vs. nonjudicial: Nonjudicial is more common, but judicial foreclosure is allowed.

Notice period: A *Notice of Default* must be filed in the county where the property is located within three months of default. A copy of the *Notice of Default* must be published once a week in the newspaper for three consecutive weeks with the last notice published at least thirty days prior to the sale date.

Right of redemption: Postsale right of redemption after judicial foreclosures.

Deficiency judgments: Allowed

Law

Title 57 Utah Code (Conveyances) Chapter 1, et seq. Mortgage foreclosures are referenced in Title 78, Chapter 37

www.le.state.ut.us/~code/TITLE57/57_01.htm
www.le.state.ut.us/~code/TITLE78/78_32.htm

Resources

Consumer Protection: www.dcp.utah.gov

Fair Housing: www.rules.utah.gov/publicat/code/r608/r608-001.htm

Landlord/tenant law: www.hud.gov/local/ut/renting/tenantrights.cfm

Local HUD Information: www.hud.gov/local/index.cfm?state=ut

Division of Real Estate: http://realestate.utah.gov/

Division of Real Estate-approved Real Estate Purchase Contract: http://realestate.utah.gov/REForms/New_REPC.pdf

Vermont
Foreclosure laws
Judicial vs. nonjudicial: Judicial

Notice period: Borrower has the right to cure certain defaults within thirty days of notice of the default.

Typical time period for foreclosure: 210–230 days

Right of redemption: Six months

Deficiency judgments: Allowed

Law
Vermont Statutes, Title 12 (Court Procedure), Part 9 (Particular Proceedings), Chapter 163 (Chancery Proceedings), Subchapter 6 (Foreclosure of Mortgages)

http://198.187.128.12/Vermont/lpext.dll?f=templates&fn=fs-main.htm&2.0

Resources
Consumer Protection: www.atg.state.vt.us/display.php?smod=8

Fair Housing: www.vtlawhelp.org/Home/PublicWeb/Pages/Housing/FairHousing

Landlord/tenant law: www.leg.state.vt.us/statutes/sections.cfm?Title=09&Chapter=137

Local HUD Information: www.hud.gov/local/index.cfm?state=vt

Real Estate Commission: http://vtprofessionals.org/opr1/real_estate

Virginia

Foreclosure laws

Judicial vs. nonjudicial: Nonjudicial

Notice period: Notice must be published at least once per day for three days, or once per week for two weeks. If the *Deed of Trust* is silent regarding notice, then the advertisement must run once a week for four weeks. If the property is adjacent to a city, it may be sufficient to advertise for five consecutive days. A copy of the notice must be served on the borrower at least fourteen days before the sale.

Right of redemption: None

Deficiency judgments: Allowed

Other: Bidders at the auction submit written, one-price bids, subject to inspection.

Law

Code of Virginia, Chapter 55 (Property and Conveyances), Chapter 4, (Form and Effect of Deeds and Covenants; Liens) inclusive of §55-48 through §55-79.06

http://leg1.state.va.us

Resources

Consumer Protection: **www.oag.state.va.us/CONSUMER/index.html**

Disclosures: **www.dpor.virginia.gov/dporweb/reb_consumer.cfm**

Fair Housing: **www.dpor.virginia.gov/dporweb/fho_overview.cfm**

Landlord/tenant law: **www.hud.gov/local/va/renting/tenantrights.cfm**

Local HUD Information: **www.hud.gov/local/index.cfm?state=va**

Department of Professional and Occupational Regulation (Real Estate): **www.dpor.virginia.gov/dporweb/dpormainwelcome.cfm**

Washington, D.C. (*see* District of Columbia)

Washington
Foreclosure laws

Judicial vs. nonjudicial: Nonjudicial is more common, but judicial foreclosure is allowed.

Notice period: Lender must send borrower thirty-day notice of default. At any time up until eleven days before the sale, the borrower may cure the default and reinstate the loan. If the default is not cured within the first thirty-day period, the trustee must send the borrower a ninety-day notice of trustee's sale, which must be recorded with the county auditor. Notice of the sale must be published in a newspaper in the county where the property is located, at least twice, at specified times before the sale.

Typical time period for foreclosure: 120 days

Right of redemption: None after a nonjudicial foreclosure. For a judicial foreclosure, there is a one-year right of redemption, and the borrower may remain in possession of the property during that time period.

Deficiency judgments: None for a nonjudicial sale. For a judicial foreclosure, deficiency may be recovered.

Law

Title 61 Revised Code Washington (Mortgages, deeds of trust and real estate contracts).

http://apps.leg.wa.gov/rcw/default.aspx?Cite=61

Resources

Consumer Protection: www.atg.wa.gov/page.aspx?id=1792

Disclosures: http://apps.leg.wa.gov/RCW/default.aspx?cite=64.06

Fair Housing: www.hum.wa.gov/FairHousing/index.htm

Landlord/tenant law: www.hud.gov/local/wa/renting/tenantrights.cfm

Local HUD Information: www.hud.gov/local/index.cfm?state=wa

Real Estate Commission: **www.dol.wa.gov/business/realestate/realestatecommission.html**

Washington State University: **www.wcrer.wsu.edu**

West Virginia
Foreclosure laws
Judicial vs. nonjudicial: Nonjudicial

Notice period: Notice must be published in the newspaper at least once a week for two consecutive weeks, and must be posted at the courthouse and at least three other public places twenty days before the sale.

Typical time period for foreclosure: 60–90 days

Right of redemption: None

Deficiency judgments: None

Other: At the foreclosure auction, the winning bidder must post one-third of the cash price at the time of the sale.

Law
West Virginia Code, Chapter 38, Article 1 (Vendor's and Trust Deed Liens) inclusive of §38-1 through §38-16-506. Deeds of Trust are referenced in §38-1-1a. Public notice provisions are set forth in other areas of the West Virginia Code, Chapter 59 (Fees, Allowances and Costs; Newspapers; Legal Advertisements).

www.legis.state.wv.us/WVCODE/59/masterfrmFrm.htm
(Legal Advertisements)

www.legis.state.wv.us/WVCODE/38/masterfrmFrm.htm (Liens)

Resources
Consumer Protection: **www.wvago.gov**

Fair Housing: **www.wvf.state.wv.us/wvhrc/index.htm**

Landlord/tenant law: **www.legis.state.wv.us/WVCODE/37/masterfrmFrm. htm** (Click on link, and then scroll to 37-6-1 and subsequent sections.)

Local HUD Information: **www.hud.gov/local/index.cfm?state=wv**

Real Estate Commission: **www.wvrec.org**

Wisconsin

Foreclosure laws

Judicial vs. nonjudicial: Judicial

Notice period: Notice of sale must be published for six weeks prior to the sale.

Typical time period for foreclosure: 365 days, unless the lender waives the right to a deficiency judgment. If the lender waives this right, the sale cannot take place earlier than six months after the foreclosure order. If the property has been abandoned, this time period is shortened to two months.

Right of redemption: One year

Law

The laws that govern Wisconsin judicial foreclosures are found in Wisconsin Statutes and Annotations (2003-2004) Chapter 846.01 et. seq. (Real Estate Foreclosure).

http://folio.legis.state.wi.us

Resources

Consumer Protection:

www.wisconsin.gov/state/app/consumer?COMMAND=gov.wi.state. cpp.consumer.command.LoadConsumerHome

Disclosures: www.wisbar.org/am/template.cfm?section=wisconsin_ lawyer&template=/cm/contentdisplay.cfm&contentid=49518

www.legis.state.wi.us/statutes/Stat0709.pdf

Fair Housing: www.fairhousingwisconsin.com/Laws_and_Remedies. htm

Landlord/tenant law: www.hud.gov/local/wi/renting/tenantrights.cfm

Local HUD Information: www.hud.gov/local/index.cfm?state=wi

Department of Regulation and Licensing (Real Estate Brokers, Salespersons, and Apprentices): http://drl.wi.gov/prof/burbiz.htm

University of Wisconsin: www.bus.wisc.edu/wcre/

Wyoming
Foreclosure laws

Judicial vs. nonjudicial: Nonjudicial foreclosures are more common, but judicial foreclosures are allowed.

Notice period: Written notice of intent to foreclose must be personally served on the borrower at least ten days prior to the first public notice. Public notices must run in the newspaper for four weeks before the sale date.

Typical time period for foreclosure: 90 days

Right of redemption: Three months after a judicial foreclosure.

Deficiency judgments: Allowed

Law

Title 34 of Wyoming Statutes, Chapter 3 (Deeds of Trust) and Chapter 4 (Foreclosure of Mortgages and Power of Sale.

http://legisweb.state.wy.us/statutes/statutes.aspx?file=titles/
Title34/T34CH3.htm

http://legisweb.state.wy.us/statutes/statutes.aspx?file=titles/
Title34/T34CH4.htm

Resources

Consumer Protection: http://attorneygeneral.state.wy.us/consumer.htm

Disclosures: **http://legisweb.state.wy.us/2007/Summaries/HB0274.htm**

Fair Housing: **http://legisweb.state.wy.us/2005/Introduced/HB0267.pdf**

Landlord/tenant law: **www.hud.gov/local/wy/renting/tenantrights.cfm**

Local HUD Information: **www.hud.gov/local/index.cfm?state=wy**

Real Estate Commission: http://realestate.state.wy.us

Appendix D

UNDERSTANDING THE REAL ESTATE CONTRACT

Using a real estate contract when purchasing a property is crucial. It defines your agreement and can both protect you from a situation gone bad, and be used to assert your position when dealing with a seller. You should buy some real estate contracts from your local office supply store, or download some from the Internet, and review them for clauses that might be important to you.

The form provided here explains the various clauses contained in a standard contract.

All sellers should be listed here, not just the person you're negotiating with. You should put your personal name in the blank as the purchaser. Another clause in the contract will let you assign the contract to any company in which you are a partner or shareholder.

Many times a real estate contract must include the legal description of the property in order to be enforceable. On the other hand, you sometimes don't know the legal description at such an early stage. To avoid misunderstandings, include as much information as you have, including the general description of the property. As general description might be one of the following: *The Seller's principal residence* or *A small office building at the corner of Oak Street and Fifth Avenue* or something similar. Be aware that street addresses and general descriptions can be misleading. A house might have one street address, but include two complete subdivision lots, with the additional lot having its own address. Or, a rental house with a detached garage apartment could have two separate addresses. When in doubt, use as many words as necessary to spell out what you're buying, and then add the legal description as soon as possible afterward. Be sure that all parties initial the legal description.

Contract to Buy and Sell Real Property

Parties. The Seller is _____.

The Purchaser is _____.

The Seller agrees to sell and the Purchaser agrees to buy the property described below.

Property. The street address of the property is _____, in the City/Town of _____, County/Parish of _____, the State of _____.

It is generally described as _____.

A legal description will be added later to this contract. The Property includes all improvements, shrubbery, plantings, fixtures, and appurtenances.

Purchase Price. The purchase price will be $_____, payable as follows:

Earnest Money. Purchaser has given the following escrow agent

_____

a check in the amount of $_____ as earnest money. It will be used as a credit against the full purchase price. In the event Purchaser fails to go through with closing for any reason, except Seller's refusal or inability to close, or one of the contingencies listed below, Seller may be paid the earnest money as liquidated damages and Purchaser will have no further liability to Seller. Seller may market the property until the date of closing and may accept "backup contracts" in order to mitigate its damages in the event Purchaser refuses or fails to proceed with closing.

Property Accepted "As Is." Purchaser is familiar with the property and any defects or problems it might have. Purchaser is accepting the property as is and will not hold Seller responsible for any repairs that are necessary after closing, as long as they've been generally disclosed here:

Don't be afraid to spell out exactly how the deal is going to be structured. If the purchase is $70,000, payable by payment directly to the lender, then say so. If it includes splitting the profits of a resale, with 80% going to you and 20% to the seller, then describe how you'll calculate whether there's a profit or not, and how large. Even if you have to include an entire worksheet by way of example, do so. It's better to be wordy and clear than succinct and vague.

It is unusual for a foreclosure purchase to include earnest money. If you're forced to put up earnest money by the lender or a seller with many interested buyers, then remember that this seller is in trouble. Don't give him or her the earnest money to keep. Pay the small fee, and name an escrow agent. It could be the lender itself, an attorney, or a title company.

This clause protects you because it forces the seller to disclose property defects. It also protects the seller because it gives him or her a safe harbor—as long as he or she discloses, you, the purchaser, assume the risk that the repairs might be more expensive than originally anticipated.

List here *anything* you might require before you're willing to completely obligate yourself to buying the property. Sample contingencies might be something as vague as: *Completion of all due diligence deemed reasonably necessary by Purchaser, in its sole discretion,* or as specific as, *Written confirmation from lender that it will accept a write-down of its debt to $70,000 and Seller's ability to transfer title free and clear of any and all claims or liens.*

Foreclosure properties present unusual risks, including the high risk that someone could record a lien at the last minute. That's why title insurance should be addressed as a completely separate contingency—you can't be sure you're safe until you reach the closing table and receive the title insurance policy.

This clause avoids all the open-ended abuses rampant in foreclosure sales. Typically, the purchaser has all the flexibility and the seller has no choice except to keep his or her fingers crossed and hope there's a closing before there's a foreclosure. Under this proposed paragraph, the parties agree on a time limit for the purchaser to do his or her due diligence. When

Contingencies. Purchaser's obligation to buy depends on its satisfaction that the following contingencies have been removed:

Title Insurance. Purchaser's obligation to buy depends on being able to secure title insurance at closing, showing that Purchaser has clear and marketable title to the property free of any liens or encumbrances (except as may be accepted by Purchaser in writing). If Seller is unable to deliver clear and marketable title, as evidenced by title insurance, then Purchaser may elect to declare this contract null and void, even if all time periods have expired for other contingencies and even if Purchaser has stated that it will proceed to closing.

Time Limit for Removal of Contingencies. Purchaser must notify   Seller   by

whether it is proceeding to closing or not, and that all contingencies have been removed if it is proceeding to closing. Notice must be in writing and there must be some sort of proof of delivery to Seller at the following address:_____

_____

_____.

Failure to give the required notice will result in Seller having the option to require Purchaser to proceed to closing, or declare the contract null and void. Seller may exercise his or her option, either to proceed or not, by delivering a notice to Purchaser by _____, at the following address: _____

_____

_____.

Notice must be in writing and there must be proof of delivery to Seller. If Seller does not give any notice by the required time limit, this contract will be null and void.

Closing. Closing will take place on or within one week afterward.

Assignment. Purchaser may assign this contract to any company, corporation, partnership, LLC, trust, or any other legal entity in which he or she holds a legal or beneficial interest.

Risk of Loss; Insurance. Until closing takes place, Seller will be responsible

the time limit arrives, the purchaser has to go *on the record* and declare his or her intentions. If the purchaser does nothing, then the seller can either force a sale or declare the contract void (at the seller's option). The seller also has to go *on the record* and give notice of his election. If neither party does anything, the contract is null and void. Typically, if the due diligence takes longer than originally anticipated, the parties should meet and agree on an amendment, changing the date for removal of contingencies.

There needs to be a deadline for closing, so the parties know if there's a default or not. If the purchaser has no time limit for closing, he or she could continue to *hang out*, claiming that he or she has every intention of buying the property, until foreclosure renders that impossible.

This clause isn't included for the purposes of *flipping* a contract. It's here to let you sign a contract with the seller and then figure out later if you want the property owned personally, or in the name of a corporation or some other legal entity. If you're intent on flipping properties, then delete the last part of the sentence that reads "...in which he or she holds a legal or beneficial interest."

One would hope the seller has property insurance, but that's not always the case. Ask for proof of insurance. Have yourself named as an additional insured, so you'll get notice if the insurance is canceled. If the seller doesn't have property insurance, ask your insurance agency if you can bind coverage for a nominal sum. Under no circumstances should you loan the borrower the money to buy insurance.

Try to find out all the normal closing costs in your area. If this is a no-equity purchase, the seller probably can't afford to pay anything at all. If it's a deferred payment for equity situation in which the seller will receive some money in the future, then spell out how the seller will pay his or her portion of the closing costs. Maybe he or she will need to bring cash to the closing table. Maybe you'll pay all the closing expenses but the seller will reimburse you through a deduction from any money you'll owe him or her in the future. If you're buying from a bank's ORE department, try to get it to pay all closing costs. Usually, you'll be successful.

for keeping the property adequately insured and for making any repairs. After closing, Purchaser will be responsible for all insurance and repairs. If Seller fails to maintain sufficient insurance and there is an uninsured or underinsured loss, Purchaser may elect to purchase the property or to declare this contract null and void. In the event of a casualty loss, Purchaser may extend the closing date, the contingency removal date, or both by a reasonable time to evaluate the extent of the damage and the adequacy of insurance coverage.

Closing Costs. Seller will pay:
$\frac{1}{2}$ of title policy
$\frac{1}{2}$ of attorney's fees

Purchaser will pay:
$\frac{1}{2}$ of title policy
$\frac{1}{2}$ of attorney's fees
All recording/filing fees

Possession. Seller (and anyone claiming under Seller or allowed to remain in possession by Seller—all of whom will be called "Seller" in this paragraph) will vacate the premises _____. If Purchaser has reason to believe that Seller will not honor its agreement to vacate by the above date, then Purchaser may close into escrow and await evidence that Seller has vacated. If Seller has not vacated by the agreed date, then Purchaser will have the option to declare this contract null and void, or it may proceed with final closing and evict Seller. In addition, if Seller has not vacated by the agreed date but the Purchaser elects to proceed with final closing, Purchaser's damages and/or costs of eviction may be deducted from any sums to become due to Seller.

Getting the former owner out of the property can be a major headache. This clause allows the Purchaser a *wait and see* time period. It also covers the situation in which the bank is the seller but the former owner is still in possession. Make it the bank's problem to get the former owner out.

Cooling Off Period. Seller has been given _____ days to consider this contract, discuss it with any advisors, and negotiate any of the terms. The resulting contract, signed by the parties, has been entered into after full deliberation and negotiation and is the full and complete agreement of the parties.

You must check your state law for the required waiting periods and for any warnings or other disclosures that must appear in contracts with sellers facing foreclosure. As written, this clause makes it clear that you aren't placing pressure on the seller to sign immediately, but honestly desire that he or she make a decision only after considering all of his or her options and their consequences.

Make sure all sellers sign. Have a third-party witness their signatures—not you. If they sign outside your presence, obtain the names and addresses of the witnesses and call them to confirm their signatures. Foreclosure is a tense, emotional time, and people sometimes do strange things. Don't take any chances. For states like California, with strong consumer protection laws in place, you might even require that the seller's signature be notarized. Whatever you do, don't witness or notarize the signatures yourself. You're an interested party and should not be a witness or notary.

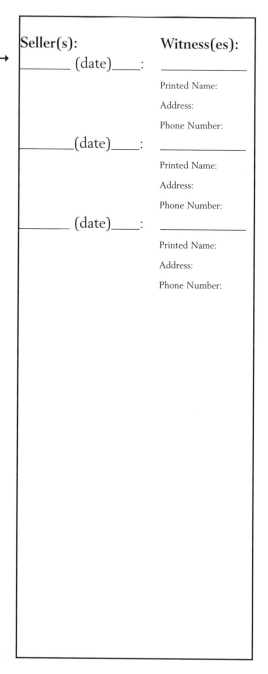

Seller(s):

_____ (date)____:

_____(date)____:

_____ (date)____:

Witness(es):

_____
Printed Name:
Address:
Phone Number:

_____
Printed Name:
Address:
Phone Number:

_____
Printed Name:
Address:
Phone Number:

SPREADSHEETS YOU CAN USE

Explanation of Real Estate Formulas You Can Use In Your Own Spreadsheets

Here are some really important calculations that will help you to analyze your investments. If you read the examples and copy the formulas into an Excel spreadsheet, you can build an impressive set of tools that will help you.

Remember these important guidelines:

1. When setting up your spreadsheet, enter values and formulas in exactly the same cells as indicated on these instructions: A1, A2, A3 and so on. Otherwise, you will need to adjust the formulas to refer to the proper cells for information.

2. All formulas should be an uninterrupted string of letters, numbers and symbols. If the instructions appear to show a space between anything in a formula, it may be because we inserted spaces in order to make the formula more readable, that is all.

3. For all loan calculations, the principal balance of the loan should be entered as a negative number. That is because the formulas rely on something called "Present Value" calculations, and your present value of a loan is always negative—you have a liability, not an asset.

	Formula 1: Calculate the monthly principal and interest payment for a fixed rate, fully amortizing loan		
	A		Example:
1		In A1, enter number of years for loan	30
2		In A2, enter annual interest rate, as a whole number	9
3		In A3, enter principal amount of loan as a negative number, and without any commas	-85000
4	=pmt(A2/1200,A1*12,A3)	In A4, enter the formula shown at left. There are no spaces in the formula. Using the example, you should receive the answer at right:	$683.93

Note: To make payments twice a month, change 1200 to 2400, and 12 to 24. To make payments bi-weekly (every other week, usually on payday) change 1200 to 2600 and 12 to 26.

	Formula 2: Calculate maximum loan for the monthly principal and interest payments you can afford on a fixed rate, fully amortizing loan		
	A		Example:
1		In A1, enter number of years for loan	30
2		In A2, enter annual interest rate, as a whole number	9
3		In A3, enter the monthly payment you can afford, without any commas	1025
4	=PV(A2/1200,A1*12,-A3,0)	In A4, enter the formula shown at left. There are no spaces in the formula. Using the example, you should receive the answer at right:	$127,388.91

Caution: Remember that lender-required escrows for taxes and property insurance, and any PMI insurance premiums for loans in excess of 80% of the value of a home, will increase your monthly payments and therefore decrease the size loan you can afford.

	A		Example:
		Formula 3: Calculate maximum loan for the every-other-week (usually, on payday) principal and interest payments you can afford on a fixed rate, fully amortizing loan	
1		In A1, enter number of years for loan	30
2		In A2, enter annual interest rate, as a whole number	9
3		In A3, enter the bi-monthly payment you can afford, without any commas	500
4	=PV(A2/2600,A1*26,-A3,0)	In A4, enter the formula shown at left. There are no spaces in the formula. Using the example, you should receive the answer at right:	$134,691.62

Caution: Remember that lender-required escrows for taxes and property insurance, and any PMI insurance premiums for loans in excess of 80% of the value of a home, will increase your monthly payments and therefore decrease the size loan you can afford.

	A		Example:
		Formula 4: Calculate the anticipated principal balance that will be due on a fixed rate loan with a balloon payment due in a certain number of years	
1		In A1, enter number of years used to calculate the amortization of the loan, such as a loan due in 20 years, but with monthly payments calculated as if it would be completely paid in 30 years.	30
2		In A2, enter the number of years when the balloon will be due, such as a 5-year balloon	5
3		In A3, enter annual interest rate, as a whole number	9
4		In A4, enter principal amount of loan as a negative number, without any commas	-85000
5	=PMT(A3/1200,A1*12,A4)	As an intermediate step, calculate the monthly payment in A4, by entering the formula shown at left. There are no spaces in the formula. Using the example, you should receive the answer at right:	$683.93
	=FV(A3/1200,A2*12,A5,A4)	Now, solve for the balloon payment that will be due in the future, by entering in A6 the formula at the left. You should obtain the answer at the right.	$81,498.12

Formula 5: Prepare an amortization schedule showing the principal and interest portion of each payment, and the loan balance due after each payment (examples follow on separate spreadsheet)

	A	B	C	D	E
1	Loan Amt:	[Enter your info]		Interest Rate:	[Enter your info]
2	Term (Years):	[Enter your info]		Monthly Pmt:	[Enter your info]
3		Monthly Payment	Interest Portion	Principal Portion	Principal Balance After Payment
4	0				=$B$1
5	1	=$E$2	=$E$1/1200*E4	=B5-C5	=E4-D5
6	2	=$E$2	=$E$1/1200*E5	=B6-C6	=E5-D6
7	3	=$E$2	=$E$1/1200*E6	=B7-C7	=E6-D7
8	4	=$E$2	=$E$1/1200*E7	=B8-C8	=E7-D8
9	5	=$E$2	=$E$1/1200*E8	=B9-C9	=E8-D9
10	6	=$E$2	=$E$1/1200*E9	=B10-C10	=E9-D10

Set up a spreadsheet exactly as above, except that you can extend it to more rows than A10. The numbers in cells A4 through A10 are the month of each loan payment, starting with month 0, on the day the loan is first made, and no payment is yet due. Month 1 (cell A5) is not necessarily January, but is the first month in which a payment will be due.

Formula 6: Compare total interest you will pay on a 15-year loan vs. a 30-year loan

	A		Example:
1		In A1, enter number of years for the 30 year loan (or whatever term you desire, as long as it is longer than A2)	30
2		In A2, enter the number of years for the 15 year loan (or whatever term you desire, as long as it is shorter than A1)	15
3		In A3, enter annual interest rate, as a whole number	9
4		In A4, enter principal amount of loan as a negative number and without any commas	-85000
5	=pmt(A3/1200,A1*12, A4)	**To solve for the monthly payment on the 30 year loan:** In A5, enter the formula shown at left. Using the example, you should receive the answer at right:	$683.93
6	=pmt(A3/1200,A2*12, A4)	**To solve for the monthly payment on the 15 year loan:** In A6, enter the formula shown at left. Using the example, you should receive the answer at right.	$862.13
7	=(A5*12*A1)-(A6*12*A2)	**To calculate the interest saved with the shorter term loan, enter the formula shown at left.** Using the example, you should receive the answer at right.	$91,031.73

To change the loan periods, such as a 20-year loan vs. a 15-year loan, just change the entries in cells A1 and A2, except that you should always put the longer time period in cell A1.

	A	Formula 7: Calculate the new loan term if you regularly make higher payments than the one required under the mortgage	Example:
1		In A1, enter number of years for loan	30
2		In A2, enter annual interest rate, as a whole number	9
3		In A3, enter principal amount of loan as a negative number, and without any commas	-85000
4	=pmt(A3/1200,A1*12, A3)	**First, you need to determine the lender-required monthly principal and interest payment**: In A4, enter the formula shown at left. Using the example, you should receive the answer at right:	$683.93
5		In A5, enter the additional amount you can pay each month, in excess of your regular mortgage payment	50.00
6	=NPER(A2/1200,A4+A5,A3)	To calculate the number of ***months*** necessary to pay the loan in full, using the higher payments you specify, enter the formula shown at left. Using the example, you should receive the answer at right.	271.63
7	=A6/12	To calculate the number of ***years*** necessary to pay the loan in full, using the higher payments you specify, enter the formula shown at left. Using the example, you should receive the answer at right.	22.64

	A	Formula 8: To calculate the additional monthly payments necessary to pay off a mortgage loan early, within a time period specified by you (such as a 30-year loan you'd like to pay off in 20-years, but do not want to chance obligating yourself to a 20-year mortgage)	Example:
1		In A1, enter number of years for loan	30
2		In A2, enter the number of years in which you'd like to pay the loan in full	20
3		In A3, enter annual interest rate, as a whole number	9
4		In A4, enter principal amount of loan as a negative number, and without any commas	-85000
5	=pmt(A3/1200,A1*12, A4)	**First, solve for the regular monthly payment**: In A5, enter the formula shown at left. Using the example, you should receive the answer at right:	$683.93
6	=(pmt(A3/1200,A2*12, A4))-A5	**To solve for the additional payment necessary each month to payoff the loan early**, in the time period specified by you: in A6, enter the formula shown at left. Using the example, you should receive the answer at right.	$80.84

Formula 9: After you've already made some payments on your loan, if you'd like to calculate the additional monthly payment necessary to pay it off early, use this worksheet. In the example below, we calculate the additional monthly payments necessary to pay off a 30-year mortgage by 20 years from now, after we've already been making payments for 10 months)

	A		Example:
1		In A1, enter the original number of years for loan	30
2		In A2, enter the number of years in which you'd like to pay the loan in full	20
3		In A3, enter annual interest rate, as a whole number	9
4		In A4, enter the current principal balance of your loan as a negative number, and without any commas. You can use a loan amortization spreadsheet to calculate this number, or obtain it from your lender.	-84,519.71
5		In A5, enter your regular monthly principal and interest payment. Using the example, it would be the number at the right	683.93
6	=(pmt(A3/1200,A2*12, A4))-A5	**To solve for the additional payment necessary each month to payoff the loan early**, in the time period specified by you: in A6, enter the formula shown at left. Using the example, you should receive the answer at right.	$76.52

Formula 10: Calculate your REAL interest rate after accounting for loan fees and treating them as prepaid interest. This should approximate the APR quoted to you by the lender. "Approximate" is the important word here, because there are no firm rules about all the items that should be included in the "loan fees" for purposes of calculating the APR.

	A		Example:
1		In A1, enter number of years for the fully amortizing loan	30
2		In A2, enter the interest rate quoted to you by the lender for a fixed rate loan	9
3		In A3, enter principal amount of loan as a negative number, without any commas	-85000
4	=pmt(A2/1200,A1*12,A3)	First, you must calculated the monthly payment for such a loan. Enter in A4 the formula shown at the left. Using the examples, you should obtain the answer at the right.	$683.93
5		In A5, enter the total of lender-charged discount points and any other fees or expenses charged by the lender and not paid to 3rd parties. An appraisal fee, inspection fee, or survey expense are usually 3rd party fees and should not be included.	2200
6	=(RATE(A1*12,A4,A3+A5))*12	To solve for the effective interest rate, being the REAL interest rate after including all up front fees paid to the lender, enter in A6 the formula shown at left. Using the examples, you should receive the answer at the right.	9.3%

Remember to format cell A6 as a percentage, with two decimal places. To do this, right-click in the cell, click on Format Cells from the menu that appears, and then click on Percentage, and then 2 decimal places.

Formula 11: If you will payoff your loan earlier than the full amortization period (because of sale of the home or re-finance) then up-front loan fees will dramatically increase your effective interest rate. Calculate your REAL interest rate after accounting for loan fees and treating them as prepaid interest.

	A		Example:
1		In A1, enter number of years for the fully amortizing fixed rate loan quoted to you	30
2		In A3, enter the interest rate quoted to you by the lender for a fixed rate loan	9
3		In A4, enter principal amount of loan as a negative number, without any commas	-85000
4	=pmt(A2/1200,A1*12,A3)	First, you must calculate the monthly payment for such a loan. Enter in A4 the formula shown at the left. Using the examples, you should obtain the answer at the right.	$683.93
5		In A5, enter the total of lender-charged discount points and any other fees or expenses charged by the lender and not paid to 3rd parties. An appraisal fee, inspection fee, or survey expense are usually 3rd party fees and should not be included.	2200
6		In A6, enter the number of years you realistically think the loan will stay in place. The average American sells their home every 5 to 7 years.	5
7	=FV(A2/1200,A6*12,A4,A3)	As an interim step, you must solve for the principal balance of the loan at the time you think you will pay it off. In this example, that will be in 5 years. In A7, enter the formula at the left. For the example numbers, you should obtain the answer at the right.	$81,498.12
8	=(RATE(A6*12,A4,A3+A5,A7))*12	To solve for the effective interest rate for the anticipated shorter loan term, being the REAL interest rate after including all up front fees paid to the lender, enter in A8 the formula shown at left. Using the examples, you should receive the answer at the right.	9.67%

Remember to format cell A8 as a percentage, with two decimal places. To do this, right-click in the cell, click on Format Cells from the menu that appears, and then click on Percentage, and then 2 decimal places.

	A		Example:
	Formula 12: Calculate the loan payoff if you pay your loan early and have a pre-payment penalty.		
1		In A1, enter number of years for the fully amortizing fixed rate loan quoted to you	30
2		In A3, enter the interest rate quoted to you by the lender for a fixed rate loan	9
3		In A4, enter principal amount of loan as a negative number, without any commas	-85000
4	=pmt(A2/1200,A1*12,A3)	To calculate the monthly payment for such a loan, enter in A5 the formula shown at the left. Using the examples, you should obtain the answer at the right.	$683.93
5		In A5, enter the number of years you realistically think the loan will stay in place. The average American sells their home every 5 to 7 years.	5
6		In A6, enter the prepayment penalty. This should be a percentage of the loan balance at the time you want to pay it off early. If the prepayment penalty is 3%, you enter 3 in A6.	3
7	=FV(A2/1200,A6*12,A4,A3)	As an interim step, you must solve for the principal balance of the loan at the time you think you will pay it off. In this example, that will be in 5 years. In A7, enter the formula at the left. For the example numbers, you should obtain the answer at the right.	$81,498.12
8	=(A7*A6/100)	To calculate the prepayment penalty, enter in A8 the formula shown at left. Using the examples, you should receive the answer at the right.	$2,444.94

Formula 13: Calculate what fees you should charge to obtain a particular yield (effective interest rate) on a loan. This is how lenders set their fees and rates, and what you should do if you will hold the financing for the sale of your property.

	A		Example:
1		In A1, enter number of years for the fully amortizing loan	30
2		In A2, enter the interest quoted interest rate for the loan	9
3		In A3, enter the effective interest rate (yield) you would like to receive	9.5
4		In A4, enter principal amount of loan as a negative number, without any commas	-85000
5	=pmt(A2/1200,A1*12,A3)	First, you must calculate the monthly payment for such a loan. Enter in A5 the formula shown at the left. Using the examples, you should obtain the answer at the right.	$683.93
6		In A6, enter the number of years when the balloon payment will be due. If you will not require a balloon payment, enter 0.	5
7	=FV(A2/1200,A6*12,A5,A4)	As an intermediary step, you will need to calculate the principal balance due when the balloon is due. In A7, enter the formula at the left. Using the examples, you should obtain the number at the right.	$81,498
8	=(A4-(PV(A3/1200,A6*12,A5,A7)))/A4 *Note: After the segment "A5,A7", that's three closing parentheses in a row and then a slash.*	To calculate the points (percentage of the initial loan amount) you should charge to obtain the yield you desire, enter in A8 the formula at the left. Using the examples, you should obtain the number at the right.	1.95%

Remember to format cell A8 as a percentage, with two decimal places. To do this, right click in the cell, click on Format Cells from the menu that appears, and then click on Percentage, and then 2 decimal places.

Formula 14: Calculate the market value of a loan. If you wish to purchase a loan that has an interest rate different from prevailing rates, what should you pay to buy that loan? If interest rates are now higher, you should pay less than the principal balance, if interest rates are now lower, you would agree to pay more than the principal balance, provided the borrower could not prepay the loan.

	A		Example:
1		In A1, enter the principal balance on the loan, as of the date of your anticipated purchase. This figure is not used in any calculations for this exercise, it's merely put in A1 for reference purposes.	-85000
2		In A2, enter the number of months remaining on the loan until maturity, assuming it is a fully amortizing loan	360
3		In A3, enter the effective interest rate (yield) you would like to receive	12
4		In A4, enter the borrower's monthly principal and interest payment	683.93
5	=PV(A3/1200,A2,A4)*-1	To calculate the market value of the loan, in order to obtain the interest rate you've specified (12% in the example), enter in A5 the formula at the left. Using the examples, you should obtain the number at the right.	$66,491

Formula 15: Convince a seller-financing mortgage holder to accept less than the full amount due to payoff a loan early, if today's interest rates are significantly higher than the rate charged in your fixed-rate, fully amortizing loan. This spreadsheet shows that a seller can accept less than the full face amount of the loan, invest that money at today's rates, and still receive the same yield.

	A		Example:
1		In A1, enter the principal balance on the loan, as of the date you wish to pay it off. This figure is not used in any calculations for this exercise, it's merely put in A1 for reference purposes.	-85000
2		In A2, enter the number of months remaining on the loan until maturity, assuming it is a fully amortizing loan	240
3		In A3, enter interest rates that can be earned on fairly safe investments, at today's rates	12
4		In A4, enter your monthly principal and interest payment	683.93
5	=PV(A3/1200,A2,A4)*-1	To calculate how much money, invested at today's rates, would return the same yield as if you kept your loan for the entire amortization period, enter in A5 the formula at the left. Using the examples, you should obtain the number at the right.	$62,114.12

Index

1031 exchange, 113, 118, 120, 124

A

accounting, 48, 65, 118, 119
activity, passive, 113, 120–122
advertising, 31, 51, 59, 60, 77, 83, 103, 135
Alternative Minimum Tax (Alt-Min), 113, 120, 121
annual percentage rate (APR), 99, 103, 104
appraisal, 7, 34, 51, 77, 82, 108
assumption fee, 86
auction, 2, 3, 6–8, 10, 11, 13, 17, 18, 29, 30, 34, 35, 47–49, 53, 54, 56, 57, 60, 61, 75–77, 79, 87–91, 94

B

bank, 12, 13, 16, 19, 20, 41, 44, 49, 57, 65, 83, 100, 107, 139, 140
bankruptcy, 2, 3, 11, 29, 42, 43, 45, 49, 73, 74, 76, 85–87, 109, 125, 127–131, 136, 138
borrowing money, 2, 42, 49, 101, 114
broker's price opinion (BPO), 7, 29, 30
budget, 31, 38, 42, 51, 60, 61, 64, 81
business plan, 25
buyer's broker, 92, 93

C

cap rate, 83, 84
capitalized income approach, 80
cash, 5, 25, 47–50, 69, 75, 83, 84, 86, 89, 101, 128, 131, 138, 142
closing company, 16, 54
closing cost, 33, 49, 86, 97, 100
comparables approach, 79, 80, 82
cost allocation depreciation, 118
cost recovery, 118
court, 6, 8–10, 21, 66, 77, 95, 129–131, 134, 138
credit, 2, 5, 8, 10, 43, 48–50, 99–101, 108, 109, 115, 117, 122, 129

D

debt, 3, 10, 50, 65, 66, 68, 74, 75, 85, 89, 108, 115, 125, 128–130, 136
debt service coverage ratio (DSCR), 50, 51
deduction, 83, 113, 115–122
deed, 1, 6, 7, 9, 10, 14, 16, 19, 31, 34, 43–45, 53, 54, 64, 66, 79, 82, 95, 96, 136–140
default, 6, 7, 11–13, 18, 23, 45, 56, 60, 64, 65, 69, 70, 94, 136–138
deficiency claim, 68
deficiency judgment, 10, 12, 13

Department of Housing and Urban
Development (HUD), 39, 40, 50,
52, 53, 55, 56, 90, 91, 101, 109,
123
depreciation, 83, 113, 116–122

E

earnest money, 8, 48, 57, 79, 89, 94, 96
equity stripping, 85

F

fair market value, 23, 41
Federal Housing Administration (FHA),
23, 40, 50, 64, 65, 72, 99, 100,
108–110
financing, 8, 34, 40, 42, 48–51, 68, 70,
79, 86, 97, 99–101, 103, 105, 107,
109–111, 133, 136–139
flipping, 25, 37, 41, 61, 68, 90, 100,
113, 114, 123, 135, 137, 139, 141
For Sale By Owner (FSBO), 28
foreclosure, judicial, 1, 6, 9, 53
foreclosure, nonjudicial, 1, 6, 7, 53
foreclosure, voluntary, 1, 10, 11

G

Good Neighbor Next Door program,
39, 40, 50, 91
government, 2, 3, 16, 39, 47, 54–57,
76, 82, 90, 129

H

holding cost, 31, 41, 140
homeowner, 22, 23, 25, 28, 37, 39, 40,
42, 47, 50, 56, 57, 59, 61, 68, 80,
90, 110, 116, 118, 123, 130, 142

I

income, 5, 13, 22, 30, 31, 43, 50, 51,
56, 57, 65, 69, 70, 79, 80, 83, 84,
86, 87, 105, 106, 108, 109, 113,
114, 116–121, 123, 125, 130, 140,
142
inspection, 8, 44, 94
insurance, 4, 13, 16, 19, 21, 23, 27,
30–34, 40, 42, 44, 50, 51, 61,
63–65, 72, 73, 83, 85–89, 97, 100,
109, 140
insurance, title, 16, 27, 31, 33, 34, 85,
87, 89
interest, 4, 5, 9, 10, 21, 25, 33, 44,
48–50, 69, 70, 74, 83, 84, 96, 97,
99–108, 110, 111, 113, 115–117,
140
Internal Revenue Service (IRS), 2, 3, 7,
14, 15, 33, 34, 55, 56, 65, 69, 74,
76, 96, 113–116, 118, 119,
121–125, 138, 140
investing, 1, 4, 17, 22, 24, 25, 27–29,
31–34, 37, 43, 44, 49, 84

J

judgment, 2, 3, 7, 10, 12–15, 29, 38, 54, 66, 68, 69, 109, 129

L

lender, 2, 4–13, 15–20, 24, 25, 29, 31, 33, 34, 41, 42, 44, 45, 47–51, 53, 60, 63–70, 72, 73, 75, 84, 86, 87–89, 91, 93, 94, 96, 97, 100–109, 113, 125, 129–131, 136–139, 141

lien, 2, 7, 14–16, 31, 33, 34, 66, 74–76, 85, 87–89, 96

lien, mechanics' and materialmen's (M&M), 14, 15

lienholder, 11, 14–16, 63, 66, 74–76, 87, 88

like-kind exchange. *See* 1031 exchange.

lis pendens, 9, 53

loan, 2, 6, 12, 13, 16, 17, 19–21, 23, 25, 33, 40, 42, 49, 50, 53, 56, 60, 63–65, 69–71, 72–74, 76, 79, 86–88, 97, 99–111, 113–115, 125, 137, 139, 140

loan, fully amortizing, 99, 105

loan, partially amortizing. *See* mortgage, balloon.

M

mortgage, 4–7, 9, 13–17, 19–21, 23, 40, 42, 45, 48–51, 53, 54, 61, 63–66, 69, 72, 74–76, 83, 84, 86, 88, 99–102, 105, 106, 110, 113, 115–117, 125, 130, 137–139, 142

Mortgage Electronic Registration System (MERS), 1, 19, 20, 64

Mortgage Identification Number (MIN), 20, 21, 120, 121

mortgage, adjustable rate, 4, 99, 101, 106

mortgage, balloon, 99, 105

mortgage, variable rate, 99, 106

Multiple Listing Service (MLS), 28, 82

N

net operating income (NOI), 51, 84, 142

O

option, 43, 49, 59, 67, 69, 106, 128

P

personal residence, 37–39

point, 4, 6, 11, 34, 44, 54, 60, 82, 90, 95, 96, 99, 101–103, 134, 141

postforeclosure, 12, 16, 21, 30, 33–35, 41, 43, 48, 49, 61, 68, 79, 90–93

preforeclosure, 7, 11, 17, 29, 30, 34, 35, 47, 48, 53, 54, 58, 60, 61, 67, 73, 79, 85, 89–91, 97, 131

prepayment penalty, 99, 104

private mortgage insurance (PMI), 40, 50, 63, 65, 69, 72–74, 86 profit, 24, 25, 45, 68, 71, 72, 75, 86, 102, 118, 138

R

real estate, 1, 2, 4, 6, 7, 9, 12–16, 19, 20, 23, 25, 29, 31, 33, 39, 41–44, 47–60, 64–66, 68, 69, 72, 75, 76, 79, 80, 82–85, 89, 91–97, 100, 113, 117–120, 122–124, 127, 131, 139, 140

real estate agent, 16, 29, 60, 66, 79, 82, 92, 93, 97

real estate broker, 7, 51, 52, 66, 84, 91, 93, 94

redemption right, 10, 21, 41, 43, 44, 68, 75, 131, 134

renting, 13, 23, 28, 30–32, 37, 39, 41–45, 50, 51, 56, 61, 68, 80, 83, 84, 89–91, 96, 100, 106, 108, 109, 113, 114, 118, 119, 121, 122, 130, 133–136, 140–143

repair, 31, 49, 51, 61, 66, 95, 119

revitalization, 39

right to redeem, 74

risk, 24, 27, 28, 31, 38, 94

S

scout, 47, 57, 58, 68

seller financing, 49, 79, 97, 138

servicing company, 17, 18, 20, 49, 60, 63–65, 70, 71, 73

short sale, 79, 87, 88, 113, 125

Starker exchange. *See* 1031 exchange.

subordination agreement, 13

subprime loan, 23, 101

T

tax, 2, 4, 7, 13–15, 21, 30, 32, 33, 42, 44, 49–51, 54, 56, 57, 61, 64–66, 69, 76, 82, 83, 88, 97, 113–125, 129, 137, 138, 140

tenant, 1, 4, 9, 13, 14, 28, 32, 42, 43, 60, 79, 86, 90, 96, 134, 135, 140–142

title, 6, 8, 16, 27, 31, 33, 34, 44, 45, 53, 54, 64, 69, 75, 85, 87, 89, 95, 96, 136, 138

V

Veterans Administration (VA), 40, 50, 52, 55, 65, 72, 99, 100, 107, 108

About the Author

Denise L. Evans received her law degree from the University of Alabama Law School, with a concentration in real estate, tax, and finance. While a law student, she served on the Board of Editors for the Journal of the Legal Profession, published two scholarly articles, was director of the Legal Research Department, and clerked with a law firm that had a large real estate practice. She graduated at the top of her class, earning the prestigious Henderson M. Somerville Prize. Afterward, she spent several years in Houston, Texas, in commercial litigation, much of it related to real estate. At the pinnacle of her legal career, she headed a specialized department of eight litigation attorneys and support staff, and conducted legal training for lawyers throughout southern Texas.

Today, she is a successful businesswoman in a variety of real estate–related businesses, including one that she sold several years ago for a profit of several million dollars. She is a licensed commercial real estate broker with a very active practice. She has twenty years of experience in conducting seminars, consulting, and passing on her secrets and insights to other people, as well as successfully implementing them herself.

Never content to rest on her laurels, she applied for, and was accepted as, a candidate for the coveted CCIM (Certified Commercial Investment Member) designation. Ms. Evans serves on the finance committee of the Birmingham chapter of CREW (Commercial Real Estate Women) and is a research associate for the Alabama Real Estate Research and Education Center at the University of Alabama. She organized a very successful merchants' association for her part of town, and serves as president.

She resides with her husband, two Chinese Pugs, a German Shepherd, half a million honeybees (really!), and assorted wildlife on forty acres of relatively blissful peace on Lake Tuscaloosa, in Alabama.